MW00414568

HE HOLDS MY HAND

by
Yuen-Lin Wu

Translated by David Wong

Buena Book Service
a subsidiary of
Horizon House Publishers
3825 Hartzdale Drive
Camp Hill, PA 17011

ISBN 0-88965-096-9

© 1991 by Horizon House Publishers

Cover painting by
Karl Foster

Contents

FOREWORD

This book is published to commemorate the faithful work done unto the Lord by the late Miss Yuen-Lin Wu. Through the long years, she consistently labored in the ministry of our Lord. Miss Wu and I have known each other and served together for many years. I can give this testimony about her:

1. Her devotion and commitment to the ministry was total.

2. It can be said that her work was the most successful among all the orphanages in Shanghai, China.

3. She suffered many trials, but was true to her faith.

4. Her work was completely dependent on faith. She did not do fund raising, trusting wholly instead on God. The orphanage grew from two children to over 300.

5. The results of her work and honest testimony have led many people to believe in God, in Jesus Christ and become Christians.

May our readers find encouragement in this book.

Keng-Sheng Shao
January, 1987

INTRODUCTION

Many years ago, my heart was deeply touched when reading the biography of George Muller of England. By ministering in the orphanage, he manifested a faith that moved men to a spirit of total self-surrender to God. God also showed His wonderful, mighty works through him.

Recently, after reading the original draft of this book, I felt the same stirring of the spirit. A thought came to mind: here is another George Muller.

My close friend, Keng-Shing Shao served as a board member of the Immanuel Orphanage at Shanghai. He is thoroughly familiar with the work of the orphanage, and of the character and spiritual life of Miss Yuen-Lin Wu. He has vouched for the truthfulness of the testimonies in this book. He has a deep respect and appreciation for Miss Wu.

At the end of this book, there is a compliment given by a neighbor of hers in Shanghai: "She and her work are a lighthouse among all of us." After reading this book, I feel that this statement is accurate.

I find in this book a person who has totally given herself to the Lord, taking the road of self-sacrifice to the end.

I find very clearly in this book the fruits of the Holy Spirit.

I find in this book the deep resolve to stand up for the Lord in times of trial.

I find in this book a person who, trusting completely in God, upholds spiritual principles. This reflects the spirit of Hudson Taylor.

I find in this book a person who, while feeble and frail in body, manifested the great power of God.

I find in this book how the love of God flowed through His servant to the orphaned, widowed, aged and weak people in China.

I find in this book a person who gave up the privilege of marriage to do God's bidding.

I find in this book how God responded to the simple faith of a person and did His wondrous and amazing works.

These words above come from my heart.

Miss Yuen-Lin Wu was endowed with the might of the Spirit and the gift of preaching the Word in Chinese and in English. She was invited by many churches and schools to preach at revival and deeper life conferences. While studying in a theological seminary at New York, she had to decline many speaking invitations offered her because of the sheer number of them. She was used greatly by God at Presbyterian, Baptist, Lutheran and Christian and Missionary Alliance churches. She was asked to remain in the United States and continue her preaching ministry, but the calling she received from the Lord was to return to China. Her obedience was most admirable.

She went through eight years of the Sino-Japanese War and many more years under Communist rule in China, but she remained faithful and loyal to the task God called her to do.

This is a book that will affect and change lives.

Philip Teng

PREFACE

"And Mary said:/ 'My soul glorifies the Lord/ and my spirit rejoices in God my Savior'" (Luke 1:46-47). "Since my youth, O God, you have taught me,/ and to this day I declare your marvelous deeds" (Psalm 71:17).

I am fully content with the love of the Heavenly Father and His wondrous works. There are times I face danger, but because God is with me, big difficulties changed to small things, and small things became nothing. The love of the Heavenly Father is as deep as the ocean, and those who trust in Him will not be put to shame. When I reflect how the Lord worked His wonderful deeds on my behalf, I wish that my whole body was one mouth to speak of His great and mighty deeds. I can never pay back even a small portion of His love for me.

There were times when the Lord told me to depend on His strength and write about His faithful works. But I lacked courage to write with these feeble hands, and I was disobedient to the Lord's command. Time flies and once it passes it does not return. I am already 80 years old, and "like a dimming candle before a blowing wind," my days on earth are numbered. But as Isaiah says, "'You are my witnesses,' declares the LORD,/ 'and my servant whom I have chosen'" (Isaiah 43:10). "'The people I formed for myself/ that they may proclaim my praise'" (verse 21). God has chosen me to be His witness and to be His servant. And a servant must obey her Master's command. This is the servant's primary duty.

The Lord has chosen me, that I may speak of His virtues. This is the command of the Heavenly Father, and it is also a duty I am obliged to fulfill. I had the desire to write this book many years ago, and my friends both here and abroad shared the same hope. Recently, I felt moved in my heart to follow God's leading, and I picked up my pen, believing that

God would take full responsibility for what I wrote.

May God bless those who read this book. May He strengthen their faith and cause them to know that in all things, they can depend on Him for victory over whatever troubles and hardships they face. I sincerely hope that those who read this who do not know the Lord will receive the illumination that will lead them to the loving Heavenly Father.

Yuen-Lin Wu

1

A Unique Status

China, like many countries of the world, used to value male babies over female ones. The more boys born to a family meant that that family was blessed and honored. It was hoped that when the boys grew up, they would become officials in the government or businessmen and be rich—something impossible for women. Girl babies brought shame to a family. After all, when they were married, they would belong to another family, another clan.

My parents' first child was a boy, something that made all the relatives happy. Afterward, my mother had three girls, all of whom died before their first birthday.

When my mother was pregnant with me, the whole family was apprehensive. Would it be a boy or a girl? What would happen if it was a girl? Would she live long?

Well, it is obvious now what the result was—a girl! My father gave much thought to the matter of a name, finally deciding on Yuen-Lin. Yuen refers to "the clouds in the sky." Lin means "deer." I know now that it is a special name, and that God had special plans for me. Otherwise, my life might have ended at an early age. I think of Isaiah 46:3: "You whom I have upheld since you were conceived,/ and have carried since your birth."

As I grew, I developed a special relationship with my father, which surprised people. He treated me as his precious jewel.

Dream prophecy

I remember a dream from my childhood, one that frightened me and, as it turned out, one that forecasted the future. I dreamed I saw a red boat docked by the side of the river near where we lived. Some of the people on the shore were wearing sack-cloth and others were wearing white. Their eyes were all fixed on the boat's deck. My mother was lying there with her eyes closed.

When I got up in the morning and told my parents about the dream, I was told never to mention it again. Not long after this, my mother gave birth again, to another girl. At the one month's birthday festivities, there was an appetizer of clams, which my mother ate. That night she became violently ill. The doctor was called, and he gave her medicine. But it did not help, and a few days later, she died.

Before she died, I remember crying out, "Mother! Mother!" I was not even four years old, and I did not understand what it meant to lose your mother. Some months later, my younger sister also died.

Where is God?

There are many incidents about my early life that I do not remember, but there is one thing I shall never forget: my father loved me dearly.

When I was seven or eight years old, three questions began to surface in my heart: Where did everything in the world come from? Where did the first human in the world come from? What was heaven like?

Of course, my family worshiped Buddha. On top of the red-wood wall in our guest room were the idol image of Buddha, an incense altar, candles and swords. At the front of the altar was a square table. On New Year's Day and other special times we were supposed to bow before the altar and burn incense. I often ran off to be by myself at these times.

As far as I can remember, I never bowed to the idol or prayed to departed ancestors. Even at that young age, I sensed that this was not worshiping the true God. Somewhere, I must have seen or heard about God, but I do not recall now. When I felt a need to pray to Him, I would wait until I was alone, then I would go behind the big door at the right of the rooftop and kneel down. I would put my hands together on my forehead and reverently say, "Father in Heaven, please do one thing for me. Please make my father come home to eat dinner."

Sometimes I asked for other things. And every time I prayed it seemed as if I received a positive response. My father would come home bringing a duck, a ham or some good things to eat. No doubt, I prayed selfishly; I wanted good food to eat. But if my father did not come home, then we had little to eat.

At the time, I did not realize that this "Heavenly Father" whom I was seeking is Creator God. He heard my seemingly insignificant prayers—"Though the LORD is on high, he looks upon the lowly" (Psalm 138:6)—and He moved the heart of my father, making him come home.

God knew beforehand that I would go through many trials and difficult times. He caused me to search for the eternal, living God who created all things.

Books to read, songs to sing

My stepmother's nickname was "Tigress," and everyone who knew her was afraid of her. Even my father dared not say much to her, fearing that what he said would lead to an unending argument. Newly hired servants did not last more than three days before they quit.

Fortunately, there was one servant, Shao-Ren, who came with my stepmother when she married my father. She was alert and talented and fitted my stepmother's temperament. Shao-Ren treated me very well, and I liked to follow her around. Wherever she went, I wanted to be with her.

But one day, she would not let me go with her. "Little Miss," she said, "you can't come with me. But I'll be right back."

She did not come right back, though. My stepmother searched for her everywhere but could not find her. At noon the next day, a detective from the police station came to our door. "Do you have a servant who is missing?" he said. "I think we have found her. I asked her why she ran away. She was ashamed to answer, but she spoke her mind, 'I want to be free.' You can go and claim her this afternoon. If I were you, I would find a husband for her and marry her off."

When Shao-Ren came home she said to me, "Little Miss, the place I've been is especially nice. There are books to read and songs to sing, but they refused to take me in. They said I am too old and will not fit in. They told me to go home and get married."

When I heard Shao-Ren talk about books and songs, I longed to see this place. *Perhaps they would accept me*, I thought.

One day I went with Shao-Ren to the marketplace. As we walked along, suddenly she called to someone in a passing rickshaw, "Miss Bao! Miss Bao!" The person was a white woman. She turned her head when she heard Shao-Ren calling and smiled a radiant smile.

I ran . . . to the school

One afternoon, my father was away, my stepmother was busy upstairs and the servant was nowhere to be seen. I was left alone and wanted to go out to play. I walked and played, walked and played and eventually ended up at the train station. I had never gone so far from home by myself, but I was having fun, and I did not want to stop. I watched in awe as the trains went by, loaded with hundreds of passengers.

It began to get dark, and I did not know what I would do. I thought about going to a friend of my stepmother who lived near the market. My stepmother often brought me to visit her, and I referred to the woman as "Auntie."

So I found my way to her house. Just as I was going to knock on the door, the servant opened it. Surprised to see me standing there, she asked, "Little Miss, how come you came by yourself?"

Several people were visiting Auntie, and they asked about me. I remember clearly what Auntie said to them: "This young lady is very smart. It is unfortunate that her mother died early." They all felt sorry for me, and someone said there was a school that did not charge for food or tuition. When I heard that, I quickly responded, "I want to study and go to school."

One person suggested that he would take me to the school, but Auntie said, "If you take her, her father will take you to court." From these words I gathered that my father really loved me and that he did not want me to leave home. But I badly wanted to go to school. Finally, Auntie said, "It is late. She needs to go home."

Auntie sent several people to accompany me. Upon reaching our house and ringing the bell, I heard my step-mother call from upstairs, "Coming!" When I heard her I knew that my father and brother were not home yet. If I went inside my stepmother would give me a terrible beating. What was I going to do?

Suddenly, I turned and ran, looking behind me every so often to see if I was being followed. It was not until I passed the meeting hall that I felt safe enough to walk. This is the first time that I had been out at night alone, and I was afraid. But I remembered the school and had heard enough of the conversation at Auntie's to piece together about where it was. I ran up and down the streets looking for it. Then I saw an old man and ran over to ask him if he knew where the school was.

"Why do you want to find the school?" he asked.

"I want to study."

"It is not a good school," he replied.

"It does not matter," I told him. "I still want to go."

So he led me to the school. Surprisingly, the people there allowed me to stay the night. When I went to bed, it was already 11:30.

Every time I remember that evening, my heart is full of praise to God. The Shanghai of the early 1900s would find few people out in the streets at night. When I was wandering around, God led this old man to pass by me. He was a principled person. If I had fallen into the hands of someone evil, it is hard to imagine what might have happened to me. But God led me directly into His sheepfold.

"Call for her father"

The next morning one of the teachers, Miss Wu, gave me a new hand towel and toothbrush. After breakfast, we cleaned up and went to chapel—a new experience for me. Later, she called me in to talk with her, and I told her everything. "Little girl, you are very smart," she said. "You spoke clearly about everything. Unfortunately, we cannot accept people with families."

After she asked where I lived, she went to report to the school principal—the same Miss Bao Shao-Ren knew. They sent a driver to my house and informed them where I was and that my father should come and take me home. After the driver left, Miss Bao received a telephone call and had to leave. Soon the driver returned and said my father would come to pick me up after lunch.

That afternoon my father arrived. He was not angry with me, and he had brought me a new pair of shoes. Again, I knew that my father really cared for me. It mattered little in most families if a girl's shoes were worn; they could do without. But my father had bought new shoes for his daughter.

Father asked me, "Yuen-Lin, do you want to come home?"

"Daddy, I don't want to go back," I told him. "I want to stay here and study."

"Would you like me to take you to Ruey-Chi's (my older brother) home?"

"Oh, yes."

Like all children, I was ready for an adventure. Besides, Ruey-Chi loved me, and I remembered eating large crabs in his house. His daughter was my playmate, and after we ate the crabs, we made butterflies out of the shells and hung them on the wall. I had fun there.

By this time, Miss Wu was standing next to my father. She told him, "Mr. Wu, I am sorry. You cannot take your daughter home today. Miss Bao had to go out, and she left word for me to tell you to please come back tomorrow. Miss Bao wants to meet you personally."

"OK," my father said, "I will come tomorrow."

The next day it was raining, and I said to Miss Wu, "My father will not come today."

"Why not?" she asked.

"He does not go out in the rain."

On the third day it did not rain, but Father did not

come. Several days passed, and Miss Bao asked her driver to go to my home and inquire about why my father had not come. When he returned, he brought sad news. My father had gone to visit his mother and aunt. He was preparing to bring me to visit Ruey-Chi. After supper he went home. At the door, he fell ill suddenly and died.

Everyone blamed my stepmother for Father's death. They knew how she fought and argued with him, often about me. She would tell my father how bad I was, but Father always took my side. After they fought, I always felt bad because he would leave our house and go sleep at Grandmother's house. Now he was gone.

During the week that I waited for Father to take me home, Miss Bao went to Chiang Bay for a Bible study with the teachers at the school there. She told them about my situation and asked them to pray that God would reveal His will about whether they should take me in.

When the driver brought the news of my father's death, Miss Bao felt that God had answered. She immediately called the principal, who came and took me to Chiang Bay Ai-Yo School.

A new experience

School was a brand new experience for me. Everything I saw and heard was completely different from my home— even my name was changed. After conferring with the other teachers, the principal, Miss Foo, said my new name was "Rung-Ling." "You should be a person who glorifies Jesus and is filled with the Holy Spirit," she told me. Of course, I had no idea about what she meant.

There was a testimony and chapel service every Saturday afternoon, and I heard for the first time about Jesus Christ. Because I was new to the school, I sat up front on a small bamboo chair.

On Sunday, I was allowed to wear my new clothes and walked with the others down the street to the Anglican church. Miss Chou, one of the teachers, put a necklace of pearls around my neck. It was beautiful, and everyone told me how nice I looked.

But in the midst of my happiness, I was suddenly reminded of my father, and I wept. Miss Chou saw me crying and asked what was wrong. I told her I missed my father. "Don't cry," she said. "I am sure your father loved you dearly, but now he is gone."

About six months later, the Lord began working in my heart, convicting me of all the wrong things I had done. I remembered stealing money from my father, stealing things to eat, telling lies and talking bad about my stepmother. I did not know then that all those things were sin. Now that I had heard the gospel message, though, I knew that I should repent and ask Jesus to forgive me. That day I knelt and asked Jesus to come into my life, and He brought wonderful peace to my heart.

My teacher gave me a New Testament and a hymnal, and I began to read the Bible. I felt that every word was special, that God was speaking directly to me. I folded the corners of the pages that contained my favorite verses. If there were two verses on a page, I would dog-ear the upper and lower corners. Slowly, my Bible began to be thicker at one corner by about an inch.

Because I was advancing so well in my studies and in my knowledge of Scripture, my teacher gave me a complete Bible. I was thrilled. As I leafed through the pages, I came to Psalm 27:10, "Though my father and mother forsake me,/ the LORD will receive me." Again, the Lord had spoken to me, and I realized how uniquely the Bible fit my life.

I grew to love God's Word. Every night before going to

sleep, I placed my Bible beside my pillow—ready to read first thing in the morning. Not only did I read it, I was determined to live my life according to its direction. This sometimes brought hateful comments from my classmates, especially when my teachers praised me for my efforts. Some of them cared little for what the Bible said, and they were jealous. But again, God's Word spoke to the situation: "Blessed are you when people insult you, persecute you . . . because of me. Rejoice and be glad, because great is your reward in heaven" (Matthew 5:11–12).

In addition to a love for His Word, the Lord gave me a desire to pray. After school every afternoon, I would not go out to play. I went to a small storage room to pray.

The younger children, of whom I was one, had to be in bed at 7:00 p.m. But the older children were allowed to stay up later to study. After this study period, there was a voluntary prayer meeting. I wanted to attend, and finally, Miss Chou agreed. Eventually, I became the leader of this prayer group. And when no teacher was available to lead the singing, I volunteered.

God gave me a heart to worship and praise Him. And truly, He had chosen me as His child: "For you created my inmost being;/ you knit me together in my mother's womb" (Psalm 139:13). After two years I was baptized.

2

God or a Husband?

After five years, Miss Foo, the principal of Ai-Yo School, returned to the United States for furlough. Before she left she had arranged for me to attend an advanced school in the fall semester. When the new principal, Miss Tai, came, the teachers told her about me. "Let me test her for half a year," Miss Tai said, "and then I will decide what to do."

Six months passed, and it soon would be time for the new school year to start. At this time, there was a civil war raging between the north and the south portions of China, and the fighting was approaching Chiang Bay. One day we heard shooting in the distance, and word came that we would have to evacuate the school. We gathered our possessions and fell in line with the stream of people traveling to Shanghai. This prevented me from starting the new school until the next year.

When I finally arrived at the new school, which was located in Sung Chiang, I was tested for my proficiency in the Chinese language and literature. I was supposed to be reading at level five, but my teacher, Miss Lee, assigned me to level eight. All the new students at this school had to learn English, but the older students could study Chinese. Of course, I was put into the English class—something that also was prepared beforehand for me by God. After I finished my second book in English, the principal asked me to tutor another student. So I learned and taught at the same time.

Later on I went to Hwei Ling School in Su Chou. After giving me a test in English, Principal Lan said I could go to the eighth grade. However, I stayed at the seventh grade level for the other courses. And because there was no seventh grade that first semester, I went to the sixth grade.

I had studied piano for two and one-half years, and I loved to practice hymns. At Hwei Ling School I had the opportunity every Sunday afternoon to go to "Hospitality Bridge" Sunday school to play hymns. There were three Sunday schools, and three piano players were needed. There were high school students at school who played the piano, but they could not play hymns well. So I was asked to play.

The discipline of God's love

As I grew older, I began to lose my desire to read God's Word and to pray, and I began to love the world and the things of the world. At revival meetings, I recommitted my life to the Lord, but after a short while I reverted back to my old self. I knew the verse, "Do not love the world or anything in the world. If anyone loves the world, the love of the Father is not in him" (1 John 2:15). But I did not have the desire to follow it. I had become a person who loved the world and was neither cold nor hot in the things of God.

Although I had changed, God had not, and He was still working in my life. One Christmas season, we had a school party. I became vain about my appearance, especially when I realized that the clothes I wore were old. One of my classmates' mothers volunteered to lend one of her daughter's silk dresses for me to wear to the party. Although I felt it was not right and I told her no, the old Adam in my heart wanted the dress. So I wore it. The next day the principal called me to her office. She told me I should not borrow other people's clothes. Through this, I knew God was convicting me of my vanity.

Also, some of my classmates liked to read novels. I had never read one, but I wanted to. One day during class the teacher gave us some self-study time. I told her, "I need to go out and get a notebook." Actually, I was going to get a novel one of the girls had loaned me.

Unexpectedly, as I was walking down the hall, a teacher called out to me, "What do you have in your hands? Let me see it." Though I had not read a word of the book, I had it in my possession—a school felony.

It just so happened that I committed this offense on a Friday, the day when the teachers and the principal meet for conference. After discussing my fault they decided to give me two major demerits. What a shock! This was my worst mistake since I had started attending school. While it may seem as if this is a minor offense, I had broken the rules. I had sinned. But more than that, I knew that I was not seeking to please the Lord wholeheartedly.

The Lord used my wrong actions to bring me back to Himself—"the Lord disciplines those he loves" (Hebrews 12:6). The Heavenly Father loved me, and He did not want me to follow the path of those who did not love Him. When I began to go the way of the world, the Lord stepped in and stopped me.

An important crossroad

One day Principal Kung summoned me to her office. She told me she had received a letter from Principal Tai of Hwei Ling School saying she wanted me to visit her immediately. I was curious, and as soon as classes ended that day, I quickly packed my bag.

But even before I had a chance to make travel arrangements, Principal Tai showed up to take me back herself. I became even more inquisitive and thought that since she had come, I might not need to go to Hwei Ling. "Do I still need to come with you?" I asked.

She nodded her head and said, "Yes." Once on the train she handed me a long letter written in English. After reading it, I could not understand how such a thing could happen. A young man I had known was proposing marriage!

The next day was Saturday, and Miss Tai had arranged a meeting with the young man, myself and my aunt and my brother Chien-Chi. Before the young man arrived, my aunt and brother tried to convince me that this was a good opportunity. "Every woman must eventually take this road," my aunt said. Evidently, they knew how I felt—that I had earlier devoted myself to the Lord and that I was determined to stick by that vow.

When the young man came, Principal Tai introduced him. We had a pleasant meeting, and we agreed to meet again the next day. Then he left. "Do not lightly regard this opportunity," my aunt said. "You should seriously consider the matter tonight. In my opinion this young man is not bad. He graduated from college at age 19. He has been a teacher of English and physical education in high school for one year. You heard how fluent he is in English when he spoke to Principal Tai. Isn't this a good match? I will come to see you again tomorrow. I hope you will make up your mind before returning to school."

My brother picked up where she left off: "Sister, I am happy for you. I heard he is an only son. It seems that his family is dependable. I hope you will not disappoint me."

The next evening we had a big meal, and afterward, we

played the piano, sang hymns and prayed. I told them, "I am young and inexperienced, so I will do as the principal wishes." They all felt I said the right thing. Though I did not know it at the time, I actually was led by God to say those words.

Principal Tai accompanied me back to school and immediately took me out to have my photo taken. I thought that this was rushing it a bit, but I thought she probably knew best.

My classmates wanted to know why I had left school, and their speculations were running wild. "Did you go back to match a mate?" they asked. "No!" I angrily responded. I blamed everything on my aunt and brother.

A few days later the young man wrote to Principal Kung. He also enclosed a letter to me. He had a good reason for enclosing his letter to me in with the principal's. The rules of the school stipulated that boys and girls were not allowed to correspond with each other. Those who broke the rule were expelled. So naturally, I did not write him back!

I returned to Chiang Bay for the New Year's vacation. For some reason, Principal Tai had decided that the marriage was not a good idea, and when the young man came to see me, she would not let him. This suited me perfectly, because I never had any intention to marry him. I was betrothed to the Lord, and my desire was to serve Him.

3

Filled with the Spirit and Called by God

In September of 1921, Pastor Hsing Pu-Sung came from Hwa Pei to lead revival meetings at the school. He preached powerful sermons, and after every message he knelt to pray. For some reason (no doubt it was the Holy Spirit), he would come every day, lay hands on me and pray, often with tears in his eyes.

God was trying to do a work in my heart, but there were several sins I would not confess. I knew if I did, I would involve my friends, and I did not want them to be punished for breaking school rules.

I also knew, though, that confession required complete honesty on my part. For me to confess halfway would have been the same as not confessing at all, and I would not have been able to obtain victory over the enemy and the fears he brought to my heart.

The revival meetings concluded, but the Holy Spirit had not finished with me. His conviction burned as a fire in my heart, and I had no peace. One October night I went to the church to pray. I was determined to confess all my sins, to pour it all out before the Lord, asking Him to forgive me and cleanse me. That also meant telling the principal and accepting the punishment. I only asked that the peace and joy of the Lord would come to fill the emptiness in my life.

I wept bitterly before the Lord and cried out to Him just as David did, "Create in me a pure heart, O God,/ and renew a steadfast spirit within me" (Psalm 51:10). That night I totally committed myself to the Lord. Although I had given in to temptation, God never deserted me. He saw my heart and knew that I truly loved Him.

Principal Tai praised my decision to confess my wrongdoings. She had been praying for me, and this was a direct answer. What amazed me the most was that she never mentioned my friends.

"Be filled with the Spirit"

A short time after this night, I received a revelation from the Lord. It was in the evening, and I had just fallen asleep. Suddenly, I felt as if I were rising up out of my bed toward the ceiling. Then I came back down and sat on the floor. After a little while, I again ascended up toward the ceiling, and as before, I came back down to the floor.

A third time, I ascended. But this time it appeared that I was passing through the ceiling to the roof of the house, and I did not come back down. At that point, I saw a gas lantern. It was so bright that it blinded me.

I woke up and called to my roommate, "Hao An, are you awake?" "Yes," she said, "I just went to bed, how could I be asleep?"

Then, amazingly, I understood the meaning of the dream: it was a synopsis of my life. The first time I had a spiritual revival was in 1915. I was 15 years old when Pastor Lip came to hold revival meetings in Sung Chiang. On the last day of his meeting, he asked at the end of the sermon if anyone wanted to dedicate herself to being used by God upon graduation. I remember feeling at that moment as if my spirit were rising. Then it slowly sank back down. This was the time when I was seeking after the things of the world.

The second time was in 1919 when I was 19. Dr. John Hogue came to Sung Chiang Church to preach. His sermon was on God calling the prophet Isaiah, "Whom shall I send? And who will go for us?" (Isaiah 6:8). I recalled what he had said, "Students, who among you, after graduation, wants to dedicate herself to the Lord, to be sent by the Lord as Isaiah was? What is there in your life that is blocking your dedication? Is it knowledge? Is it name and reputation? Is it the world and worldly things? Is it the good things in coming days? Is it friends?

"Whoever has the desire to serve the Lord, let her come up here and express it." I stood up and went to the front, rededicating myself to the Lord. That was the second time my spirit went upward. But afterward, I came back down—this was the time when I was proposed to.

And, of course, the third time was the latest revival meetings. I knew now that this instance was more sincere and decisive than the first two. I humbly repented, confessed my sins and wholeheartedly dedicated myself to the Lord.

I also understood the meaning of the gas lantern. The lantern gave out light because it was filled with gas. When it is full the light burns brightly. But when it is low, the light is dim. The lantern is the Christian, the gas is the Holy Spirit. Christ's disciples cannot give off light by themselves. They need the Spirit of God.

Certainly, this was the Lord speaking to me: "You must seek to be filled with the Holy Spirit so that you depend on His power to prevent you from falling. Trust in the Spirit to give out a great light, then shine it forth to people all around you. Otherwise, you will revert back to your old way of living."

Right about this time, another school needed two teachers. Principal Tai was thinking of giving another new teacher and me a training opportunity. She was looking ahead to the day when she soon would head up Kan Su School, and she was thinking of taking the two of us with her. But one night the Lord said to me, "You should not go to the school. The other student can go with someone else. In the future you will go a separate way. You must first seek the filling of the Holy Spirit. Stay and minister here." The next day I told Principal Tai about the message, and she agreed that I should not go.

On New Year's Day, I went to a church at Su Chou for a revival meeting. I planned to use my vacation time to concentrate on seeking the Holy Spirit. On the evening of February 6, 1922, God's Spirit filled me with His presence!

As a fresh breeze from heaven, He came rushing into my life, and I was empowered inside. Every day, aside from work, I concentrated on seeking the Lord's face. I asked Him to help me glorify Him in everything I did. I went to the chapel every evening and prayed there alone. Leaning on His strength I dedicated my all on the Lord's altar.

From then until now, the Lord has been my everything. Not once has He failed to meet my needs. Not once has He failed to comfort me when I was sad. There was no hardship that He did not bear. I love to repeat the words of Paul: "Sorrowful, yet often rejoicing; poor, yet making many rich; having nothing, and yet possessing everything" (2 Corinthians 6:10).

That year on a Sunday in April, I went alone to the chapel just prior to the worship service. As I sang my favorite chorus "Where He Goes, I Will Go," the Holy Spirit told me, "You will serve Me in the inland."

I tearfully said, "Oh, Lord, I am willing to go, but I do not know a single person in the inland, and I do not know how to speak their dialect. How can I go?"

Again He said, "You will serve Me in the inland."

Then I knew that was my destination, and I said, "Lord, I am willing to follow You."

It sounds strange, but when the pastor preached that morning, I already knew every word he would say. This fully convinced me that it was the Lord's will for me to go inland.

God works through me

The Lord's blessings kept coming. One of the students became sick with tetanus, and she had a raging fever. One night I was moved by the Spirit to lay hands on her and pray. The next morning she was fine. After this, Principal Tai gave me an English name, "Joy." "You are God's Joy," she told me. "You laid hands on the girl, and God healed her. He is with you."

On another occasion I was invited by the chairman of the board of directors of the mission to spend a few days in her guesthouse. On the second morning, I woke up early and the Lord told me that I was supposed to go that day and teach a student Chinese in the absence of her teacher, who was sick.

When I went to eat breakfast, I found that the chairman was sick. Her sister told me, "She is asking for you to come and pray for her." So I did. As I knelt down beside her bed, she took my hands and placed one on her head and the other on her stomach.

After praying with her, I went to the student's house. She was surprised but happy to see me. She showed me a note that she had just received that said her teacher was ill and could not come to teach her. At the moment I arrived, she was praying for God to send someone else.

"I knew even before you did that your teacher was ill," I told her. "The Holy Spirit told me this morning and sent me to teach you."

She clapped her hands and said: "Praise the Lord!" and we started immediately. That afternoon we went to church for a special service. When we arrived, we saw the chairman—she was completely healed!

This was not my ability but God's. Before Christ ascended to heaven, He promised the disciples that they, too, would be able to heal the sick (Mark 16:18). Was I not also a disciple?

4

The Lord
Takes Me Inland

Four months after God called me to go inland, a German missionary came and stayed at the guesthouse of the chairman of the board of the mission school. During the morning prayer meeting, she asked those in attendance to pray that God would supply a teacher for her school—in the inland. The chairman told her about me.

That afternoon she traveled to Chiang Bay to meet me. As soon as we met and she explained the situation, I knew this was God's call, and I agreed to go. At a farewell dinner at the chairman's home, my friends and spiritual mentors came to say goodbye. Among them was Principal Foo, the person who first took an interest in me. She praised God for all that had happened in my life. When she first met me, I was a young girl who hungered and thirsted for truth. Today I was a woman on my way to teach other Chinese about Jesus Christ.

When our boat arrived at Han-Koh, we transferred to a train to travel to Chu Ma Tien. We stayed overnight at the Chiu-Un Church and the next day boarded a carriage to Pi-Yang County, a three-day journey of 180 miles. All along the way, we had to get out of the carriage when it came to a river crossing, take off our shoes and walk across while the driver negotiated the carriage through the water.

I could not believe I was actually on my way inland. At times during the first day, I did not know if I was going to have the strength to make it another mile. And when we stopped to rest for the night, I wondered how I would make it another two days. I could only ask the Heavenly Father to strengthen and to give me joy to endure the journey.

Finally, we arrived at Pi-Yang. A group of believers welcomed us, and though I could not understand their dialect, I knew they were glad I was there.

I could hardly walk after the journey. Both of my feet were cut and bruised from walking through the water crossings. Three times a day I had to wash the cuts, which in itself was a painful experience. Because I had to stay in bed, the students came to my room for their classes.

But I was determined, with the Lord's help, to get on my feet. The students were depending on me; I was supposed to teach the physical education and music classes. So one morning I decided I did not care anymore about the pain and the bleeding. I took a deep breath and got out of bed. As I stepped down, the pain took my breath away, and I cried out. *Surely,* I thought, *these wounds will heal soon.* "Jesus," I prayed, "please touch my feet."

As I started down the hallway, another teacher saw me. "Teacher Wu," she said, "I heard you cry out. I know the pain must be unbearable. But now you do not look as though your feet hurt. What has happened?"

"Before I started on my journey here," I told her, "someone gave me two dollars. I purchased five small pictures of Christ on the cross and framed them. I gave four away and kept one for myself. As I looked at that picture today, I was reminded of the pain Jesus endured on the cross. When I realize how great His pain was, mine is insignificant. There is no comparison. I had to get up and teach my students—for Jesus."

Soon after this my feet were healed completely. I am reminded of First Peter 2:24, "by his wounds you have been healed," and also of Isaiah 53:5, "the punishment that brought us peace was upon him,/ and by his wounds we are healed."

Truly, God is our healer. Not long after my feet healed, I fell and twisted my right ankle. It was so bad, I could not walk and had to be carried upstairs to my room. The students and teachers told me, "Do not come down for tomorrow morning's exercise. Stay in bed." But I prayed and asked God to heal my ankle.

The next morning, even before the alarm sounded, I was out of bed. I walked downstairs and woke up my students. When they saw me up and walking about, they were amazed. "Teacher Wu, how did you come downstairs?" they asked. Then they examined my leg—there was no swelling and the bruise had disappeared! God again had answered my prayer.

Someone was unhappy with my work

The rules at Pi-Yang Girls School were strict, and the students' course load was heavy. Because the school lacked enough instructors, the teachers also had a busy schedule. I got up at 5:00 in the morning and was busy until the evening. Except for a noon to 2:00 break for meals, there was no free time in the day.

Every afternoon after lunch, Missionary Pang wanted the teachers to walk with her. I excused myself because I wanted to spend the time in prayer.

Although I did my best to teach all my subjects well, I did not always feel confident that I was successful. Besides that, I felt most of the students did not have a proper attitude about God. How then could I point them on the right path? I decided to start a prayer meeting and opened it to anyone who wanted to come. Little by little, attendance grew as the Holy Spirit worked in the girls' hearts. Often our times of intercession lasted until dawn, yet the students continued to come.

Even other teachers joined the group. Teacher Lee Kwei-Tsang told me, "We have never had prayer meetings like these. God is truly working." To me, this was God fulfilling what I had asked for, bringing into completion His calling me to the inland.

But someone was not pleased with our prayer times—Satan! When God is at work, so is Satan. One night while we were praying, I suddenly experienced an attack of pneumonia. My condition deteriorated quickly, and I was bedridden. I knew what was happening—Satan was trying to kill me. He was displeased with my devotion to God, and he wanted to destroy me.

I was sick for a month. There were no doctors or medication, and no relief in sight. We prayed, but God did not heal. Perhaps as He did with Job, the Lord was testing my resolve.

When my condition worsened, I desired to see the Lord's face. Just as Paul, I said: "I am torn between the two: I desire to depart and be with Christ, which is better by far" (Philippians 1:23).

At last my fever subsided, but I was weak and could hardly eat. One day I felt I had to get out of bed; I was itching all over. I called for a student to come help me. When I got up, she checked the bed—it was full of lice! With tears in her eyes, the student said: "Teacher Wu, if you were in Shanghai right now, you would not be in such a state!" As she cleaned my bedding, I sang the chorus:

> Where He goes I will follow,/ Where He is, I
> will keep company,/ I will follow the Lord to the end

of the journey,/ Daily I will follow the Lord Jesus.

A great revival meeting

Pastor Hsing Pu-Sung, whom I mentioned earlier, was delighted when he found out I was at Pi-Yang, and he wanted to come visit me. Missionary Pang, knowing how God had used him in my life, wrote and invited him to come to our school and hold revival meetings. He agreed.

On the day before the meetings were scheduled to begin—and after a number of church leaders from surrounding towns had come—we received a telegram from Pastor Hsing telling us he could not come. "All these people have arrived," I told the Lord. "What will we do? They came expecting to hear a word from You, to be filled with the Holy Spirit, so they could return to their churches and feed their people."

Then it seemed as if the Holy Spirit whispered in my ear, "Was there a pastor leading the disciples when they were waiting for the coming of the Holy Spirit at Pentecost?" *So what if Pastor Hsing cannot come,* I thought then. *We can still have a revival meeting, just like Pentecost.*

At that moment someone knocked on my door. Missionary Pang came into my room and said, "Shall we have prayer?" I used the opportunity to tell her what the Lord said to me, and we prayed that the Lord would send His Spirit, that revival would break out. And He answered me with a Scripture verse: "Before they call I will answer;/ while they are still speaking I will hear" (Isaiah 65:24).

That night at the prayer meeting the Holy Spirit moved mightily. All who had come for the meetings were in attendance, and we stayed until morning! The Holy Spirit of Pentecost fell upon us.

Teacher Lee Kwei-Chan, a person for whom I had been praying, was in attendance, and the Lord met her in a powerful way. She was the first one to be filled with the Holy Spirit, and she confessed and repented of her sins, pouring out everything before the Lord.

One of the men who had come in for the meetings also received the Holy Spirit. He had never preached before, but on the second day he was invited to speak at the morning worship service. Every word he spoke was filled with the power and might of God. The revival continued for several weeks. At school, before meals, after meals, during the 10-minute recesses, the school was filled with the sound of songs and praises to God.

Acquiring the attitude of Christ

Admittedly, life was hard at the inland school. In addition to the long hours and multiple responsibilities, food was scarce and simple. In the first year, with the exception of two times I was invited out to eat, I did not have rice to eat. Noodles were the staple of the people of this area, and I learned to like them. I could eat four big bowls every meal.

I was, however, better off than the others financially because my salary was higher. Here again, I wanted to honor God in my actions. When I first dedicated myself to God, I also promised to give Him 10 percent of whatever I had of monetary value. Later, when I was filled with the Spirit, out of thanksgiving to God I voluntarily increased my giving from 10 to 20 percent.

After I started at the inland school and saw how needy some of the students were—several could not pay their monthly boarding expenses—I decided to give 50 percent of my salary to the Lord. That money was used as a fund to help needy students pay their room and board. The Lord led me to give from the other 50 percent of what I made to help those who could not pay for their monthly food expenses.

After I contracted pneumonia, someone encouraged me to buy some eggs. One dollar could buy 100 eggs, and four young hens also could be purchased for one dollar. But I did not regard this as important. I was trusting on the Lord, who told us:

> So do not worry, saying, "What shall we eat?" or "What shall we drink?" or "What shall we wear?" For the pagans run after all these things, and your heavenly Father knows that you need them. But seek first his kingdom and his righteousness, and all these things will be given to you as well (Matthew 6:31–33).

Whatever I did, I tried to glorify the Lord in it. But often I found the old Adamic nature trying to take control. For example, I caught myself saying, "Out of 365 days—except for the times I was sick—I have never been late to class. That is not an easy accomplishment!"

Paul said, "Your attitude should be the same as that of Christ Jesus" (Philippians 2:5). Sometimes I asked myself, "How can I always have the same attitude as Christ?" Again, Scripture brought the answer: "I have been crucified with Christ and I no longer live, but Christ lives in me" (Galatians 2:20). This was the way to have the same attitude as Christ.

I learned that I had to depend on the Lord's grace to be crucified with Christ daily. The attitude of Christ is never boastful, never proud, never self-seeking; it is the opposite of the Adamic nature.

5

God Leads Me Away— and Back Again!

The life of the Lord is spiritual food. "'My food,' said Jesus, 'is to do the will of him who sent me and to finish his work'" (John 4:34). Summer came at Pi-Yang, and the missionaries prepared for vacation in the mountains. Everyone told me that this would be a great opportunity for me to return with them to Shanghai.

However, Missionary Pang told me she did not want me to go. She even postponed the date of final exams two weeks so that I would have to stay and finish the term. She said she would rather give up her own vacation and keep me company than for me to go to Shanghai.

The group was set to leave very early one Thursday morning, something necessitated by the method of travel: ox carts. The carts had to leave that early in order for them to make it to a certain place on the journey. Travelers would not think of being on the road at night for fear of robbers.

The night before they were to depart, a heavy rain began to fall. Plans for leaving the next day were canceled. The rain stopped the next morning, but it was too late for them to start the trip. So they made plans to leave on the coming

Monday morning. Sunday night they packed their cases—to no avail. Again, the rain came.

Finally, the missionaries concluded that they should obey the will of the Heavenly Father and abandon their plans. They knelt down before God, asking Him to reveal why they could not begin their journey. While they were praying, the express mail brought the answer. One letter was addressed to the church leader, one to the leader of the school, another to missionary Pang and one was for me. The contents of the letters were the same: they asked for me to come to Shanghai.

Though I did not know why, I felt as if the Lord wanted me to leave. Probably, Missionary Pang sensed that I might not come back to the school, and that is why she did not want me to go. But my health was failing. I had cramps in my hands and legs, my complexion was pale, and I was vomiting blood. A missionary nurse who happened to be in the area gave me a check-up. Her diagnosis confirmed the decision for me to leave: "She should return to Shanghai immediately. The atmosphere here is not good for her."

The next day I left for Shanghai with the missionaries. As my first trip out, this one, too, proved a strain on my already poor health. Every time the cart (I was provided my own cart) hit a bump, my hands shook uncontrollably. Because the rain had made the road muddy, it was harder for the ox to walk, and at one point my cart toppled over.

At last we reached Shanghai, and I had a joyful reunion with all my friends. The second day after I returned, however, I encountered another problem—a spiritual one.

There was a new student in the school whose name was Mei-Li. When she was young, her parents had dedicated her to Buddha. Sometime before she came to the school, she was possessed by the devil. Often, she would be thrown to the floor, and she would be uttering nonsense.

Because I wanted to help her, I let her stay in my room. As

we prayed for victory, eventually the Lord cast out the demon.

The Lord comforted me

I stayed at Shanghai and began the fall term teaching at Ai-Yo School. I taught arithmetic and language in the morning, and in the afternoon I taught the missionaries Chinese. I also helped in the principal's office with correspondence and translation work.

During the spring of 1924, I again was stricken with pneumonia. This time I was so sick that the missionaries had to spend the night with me. They were afraid to send me to the hospital, fearful that something might happen to me on the way. The doctor from the Shanghai Westgate Women's Hospital came to visit me daily.

After I recovered, the principal sent me to the hospital for a thorough check-up to see if the doctors could discover what was causing my problems. In my room at the hospital I pulled out my copy of *Holy Light Daily Devotional*. I turned to the entry for that day and read a passage from Mark: "Take courage! It is I. Don't be afraid" (Mark 6:50). Instantly, peace filled my heart, and I knew that the Lord wanted me to come to the hospital.

When I finished with the devotional, I opened my Bible to a passage in the Psalms. Here again, the Lord reassured me: "precious is their blood in his sight" (Psalm 72:14). *Blood signifies life*, I thought, *and life is precious in God's sight. He would not lightly take away my life.*

The next morning I felt completely whole. It was hard to believe. I went to the bathroom by myself. The people in the ward asked in wonder, "How did you get well so fast? When you came here yesterday, we were afraid you were going to die."

Immediately, I began collecting my things, hoping that the doctors would allow me to go back to the school. But they would not, and I ended up staying in the hospital for a month and a half. I felt I was well enough to leave; they wanted me to stay and rest.

A few days after I arrived at the hospital, a nurse came to see me. She knew that I was a Christian, and she told me she wanted to know the truth about God. We talked and prayed together, and she invited the Lord into her heart. After this, the hospital invited me to preach on Friday evenings to the entire nursing staff.

Finally, the doctors said I could go home. They did not find anything wrong with me, and they would not take any payment for their services. They did, however, tell me that I should leave the Shanghai area and go somewhere to rest. The humid climate there was not suitable for my health.

Principal Tai took the doctors' advice and sent me away for summer vacation with two missionaries. We went to Cock Mountain, but after being there for only one week, I fell sick again with a high fever. They quickly called for a doctor, who determined that I had a relapse of pneumonia. He said I should leave immediately.

Never had I been more discouraged. I cried out to God, "Oh, Lord, I have dedicated my life to you. Why am I sick so often? This does not bring glory to You."

And in His still, quiet voice, He answered, "Child, do not be afraid. You will be healthy one day. When the resurrection power comes into your sick body, all your illness will disappear. Wait on Me."

God used me greatly

Since leaving Honan's Pi-Yang Girl's School, I had often thought of the students. Missionary Pang wrote me numerous times inviting me to come back. But because of my health, I knew this was impossible.

The Holy Spirit would not let me forget the school, though. The calling seemed to burn within me. I related to Principal Tai my desire—to suffer for the Lord, sacrificing myself in the valley of the shadow of death if need be. She realized that this was my life's goal.

In the spring of 1926, God led me to Enmore Girl's School to take some remedial courses and some advanced piano instruction. Upon arriving, I started a prayer meeting with a few of the students. One day a student opened the door of the room where we were, and when she heard the sound of prayer, she quickly left. After we were through she came up to me and said, "Teacher Wu, I have never heard such a prayer meeting. Can I attend?"

"You are welcome," I told her.

Soon our meeting attracted the attention of the school's principal and the other teachers. Eventually, it expanded into a public prayer meeting. God was at work.

One morning at worship service, Principal Sze asked me to lead the prayer. To God's glory, my prayer shook the hearts of many people. At the recess break, I was surrounded by the students. Some said, "We were afraid when you prayed. It was as if God had come down into our midst." Later, someone suggested to the principal that I should lead the revival meetings. She asked me, and I agreed. The outcome produced good spiritual fruit.

One student named Lee had just transferred to the school. Her past principal and teachers urged her to receive Christ as her Savior on a number of occasions, but she never did. After the revival meetings one day, she sought me out. The Holy Spirit convicted her of her sins, and she repented and accepted the Lord.

That Saturday she returned to her former high school and told the principal the good news. Her principal asked her why she believed, and the student told her about the revival meetings. Soon, I got a note from that principal inviting me to preach during their spring vacation. Again, the Lord blessed my words, and people's hearts were changed.

During summer vacation, the principal of Chiang Bay asked me to preach revival there. I was afraid to commit, but the Lord gave me a promise: "My word that goes out from my mouth:/ It will not return to me empty" (Isaiah 55:11). From this I realized that the sermons I preached were not mine; they were the Lord's words. He was responsible for the results. All I had to do was be obedient.

The meeting was successful, and I was invited to speak at other revival meetings. Principal Sze told her sister-in-law, who was ministering at Hai-Feng School, about me, and she invited me to preach. Then the two schools in Shanghai wanted to have revival meetings. I followed the Lord's leading and returned to Shanghai to lead revival and preach.

Return Inland

The most valuable experience in my life occurred the summer of 1926. During one meeting, the Lord met me in a special way. He told me that I should return inland. "Are you not afraid you will get lice again?" someone asked. "Why do you have to go?" "Because the Lord has called me," I responded, "and like Paul, I want to consider everything as loss in order to gain Christ." That fall I traveled to Pi-Yang. It was a joyous reunion. On the first day of school there was an evening prayer meeting, and the students came voluntarily. And this time, I could speak their dialect!

My trip was voluntary, and I did not receive any compensation; I even paid for my own boarding expenses. The rest I used to help those who could not pay for their boarding expenses. One student who received this support told me, "Teacher Wu, when I graduate I want to come to see you in

Shanghai. If I don't have the money, I will crawl all the way there!" She later received Christ as her personal Savior.

Although I did not get as sick this time as I did the first, I did contract bronchitis—something that stayed with me until late in my life.

Fulfilling God's word

The school year passed quickly, and in spring I began wondering what I would do for summer vacation. One morning as the students were taking their mid-term compositions, the Lord spoke and told me to go back to Shanghai. "Lord, that can't be!" I replied. "I've only been here for six months. I cannot go back now. The soonest I can leave will be summer vacation." But God insisted, "Tomorrow you will receive a letter urging you to return."

That night Missionary Pang came and said to me, "I would like you to lead the worship service tomorrow." I agreed immediately. While I was preaching the next day, the Lord continued to impress upon me about leaving. When the service was over, two students came and said, "Teacher Wu, there is a letter for you from Shanghai." It was from the missionaries, and they were requesting that I return as soon as possible.

I went to see Missionary Pang. When she saw the letter in my hand, she asked, "Is it good news?" I told her what the Lord had said to me last night and then showed her the letter. She told me that there was no money available to send me back.

The next Tuesday I received a registered letter. In it was a check for $50—my travel fare. In November I had received a letter from Shanghai. It mentioned money, but there was no check enclosed. Evidently, the sender forgot to put it in. Now it came, thanks to God who knows everything. He knew that if I had received the money earlier, I would have spent it on something else. Now I could make arrangements to leave.

After three days of traveling I reached Chu Ma Tien. The leader there, Missionary Kurt, welcomed me gladly because I could help her resolve her need of a preacher. Earlier she had invited a pastor to come and speak. Because the trains could not get through, he was unable to come. My arrival was her answer to prayer. The meetings began on Sunday and lasted until Friday.

After the meetings God reminded me that it was time to move on. Indeed, that evening someone came and said, "There is an opportunity for you to continue your trip tomorrow." Though there were no passenger trains running, I could get special passage on a military train. Once again, I was on my way to Shanghai.

By the time I arrived, the whole school was wondering where I had been and if I was all right. Someone told me there was a letter from Pi-Yang. When I opened it I read that bandits had come to the city. They went to the school looking for me because they thought I had money. Actually, I had given all my money to other people. When I reached Shanghai, I only had 20 cents left. Once again, I saw the Lord's providence in directing my life.

6

God Takes Me
to America

After I returned to Shanghai in 1927, Principal Tai mentioned that she would like to send me to America for further studies. Without hesitation, I replied, "Thank you, but I cannot go." Earlier, I may have had the desire, but since I had dedicated myself to the Lord, my sole purpose was to do His will. Reinforcing this, one night after dinner I sat down to play the piano. As I worked through the scales, the Holy Spirit began to guide my fingers and gave me a simple melody. Then, as I completed it, He also gave me the words:

> Jesus left His throne for me,/ He came to earth and became a man born in a manger./ He suffered in this world for me./ Jesus bore the cross for me, He went to the high mountain called Calvary./ He was nailed there to a cross, dying for me./ Jesus' precious blood flowed for me,/ He redeemed my sins, that I would no longer be lost./ He redeemed me, set me free and leads me./ I am willing to follow my Savior,/ To deny myself and take up the cross./ I go to save people,/ That they not perish but have

everlasting life./ Very soon my Lord will come to earth again,/ He will receive me to heaven to enjoy eternal blessings./ There when I see the face of the Lord, what joy sublime.

Later, when I played the piece for some people, they appreciated it so much that they asked me to write it down. They took it and had several thousand copies printed, which they distributed to the churches in Shanghai.

I resumed my teaching duties at Ai-Yo School, and I often substituted for the principal in leading the morning chapel services. Sometimes, I also led the Sunday worship services. Additionally, in the summers I led the school's revival meetings. Principal Tai assigned me these important responsibilities because she knew that I received my messages from the Lord.

My outside speaking engagements also increased, and gradually I felt the Lord prompting me to preach full-time. His words from Scripture seemed to confirm the inner urgings: "I have placed before you an open door that no one can shut" (Revelation 3:8).

God also confirmed the call through the meetings themselves. For instance, I preached at the Nan-Shiang Wesleyan School for a week. But because of God's mighty outpouring of His Spirit, the meetings were extended a week. Then at the end of those seven days, the principal and teachers asked me to stay two more weeks!

Songs in dreams

Late one night in 1928 I woke up singing a song. Not only did I wake up, but those next to me and across the hall were also awakened. I often sang in my dreams, so my fellow teachers were not surprised. However, this occasion was different.

When I woke up my face and night clothes were wet from crying. As I began to think about the dream and the song I was singing, I could remember the melody but not the words. I so wanted to remember them that I got down on my knees and asked the Lord to bring them back to my mind.

He did. Word by word the lyrics came, and this is the song:

> I want to love You Jesus, You are my Savior./ You delivered me from sin and made me free./ I should love You Jesus, You are my friend./ You said there is purpose in sorrow and in joy./ I truly love You Jesus, You are my everything./ I am content in You as I joyfully journey heavenward.

Along with the words, the Lord gave me the meaning of each stanza. First, "I want to love you Jesus." Christ completed the initial work of salvation, delivering me from sin. I received freedom, and Jesus became my Savior. Second, "I should love you Jesus." Not only is He my Savior, but He is my best Friend. Although I did not understand why I had to experience sickness and pain, the Lord promised that one day I would know. "And we know that in all things God works for the good of those who love him, who have been called according to his purpose" (Romans 8:28).

The third stanza is "I truly love you Jesus." What else is there aside from the Lord that is deserving of our true love and devotion? Psalm 73:25 says, "Whom have I in heaven but you?/ And earth has nothing I desire besides you." The Lord is everything to us. What more do we lack? Does everything not include our smallest needs? As we journey heavenward, we are enthusiastic and joyfully press toward the finish line.

The next morning Principal Tai asked me to speak in chapel. What better topic than last night's dream song!

Going abroad for further study

In November 1931, I attended a memorial service for a friend who went to be with the Lord. During the sermon, the Lord's Spirit began speaking to my heart. Suddenly, I recalled the words Principal Tai had spoken several years before concerning going to the United States for study. "Not only will I use you to testify of Me and to preach," God said, "I also want you to nurture people so that they will serve Me. But before this happens, I want you to travel to America for further studies."

After the service, I rushed back to the school. I entered my room and fell on my knees before God. "Lord," I pleaded, "what is this all about? Where would I ever get the money to study in America?" These and other questions rushed out. Principal Tai had asked me if I wanted to go and study. No doubt she hoped that one day I would assume a leadership position in the mission schools. But if the Lord was calling me to start a different ministry, what could I tell her?

Then the Lord brought to mind some money that I had in my dresser drawer. It had been given to me as a gift, and it was a small amount, but it was a start. Again, God spoke to me: "You can trust me. I will bring this to pass within three years." Early the next morning, God spoke again confirming the call: "Anyone who has faith in me will do what I have been doing. He will do even greater things than these." When I opened the Bible, right before my eyes was that verse, John 14:12.

Later, I wrote a chorus based on my call, using the tune of "Oh, Lord, I believe."

> You called on Me, I answered you,/ And told
> you the things you did not know./ You called on Me,
> and I answered you,/ And told you great and

unsearchable things (Jeremiah 33:3).

Time seemed to fly by, and the night before the first day of the third year, I prayed: "Oh, Lord, please give me a promise." Early the next morning, I got dressed quickly and began my devotions. I opened the Bible and there was the word of the Lord: "Wait, my daughter, until you find out what happens. For the man will not rest until the matter is settled today" (Ruth 3:18). The word "today" stood out. I took it to mean that year. So I resolved to trust in God's promise that in three years I would be able to go abroad.

As I planned to leave, one of the things I dreaded most was submitting my resignation to Principal Tai. If she refused, a misunderstanding might arise and it would not bring glory to the Lord's name. Finally, I approached her. "Please forgive me," I said.

"What for?" she replied.

"Sometimes when you introduce me to new people, you seem to suggest that I've committed my life to serve in this school."

Knowing what I was implying, she said, "Where are you going?"

"I'm going to study in America."

"It is true," she said, "that God has given you the gift of preaching. But don't you think you should wait a little longer to start? Missionary Ming waited for seven years before she embarked on her ministry."

Again the next morning, Principal Tai discussed my plans with me and tried to dissuade me from leaving. Not having any success, she finally said, "You cannot go unless God prepares another person like you who has two important gifts: preaching and administrative abilities." She wanted me to understand that there was no one to replace me among the Western missionaries or among the other teachers. Therefore, under no circumstances could I leave.

I said nothing, but later God again spoke to me: "If you obey My command then I will fulfill My promise." Now I did not know what to do. If I obeyed God, it would upset Principal Tai, and I did not want that. But God kept after me, and I continued asking for signs. "Lord, if You want me to go, please do this thing for me." After He answered, I became fearful. I asked for another sign, "Oh, Lord, if You want me to do this thing, please do this and do that." What I asked for, He delivered. I knew I had no other choice but to obey His leading.

When I again approached Principal Tai, I encountered anger as if it came from hell itself. She gave me a tongue lashing and left in a huff. Afterward, I asked another missionary, "Please pray for me. I am in trouble. I have offended Principal Tai!" I told her what had happened, and to my surprise, she thought I did the right thing.

Waiting for me back in my room was a letter from Principal Tai. Her anger came out in the words she wrote. She accused me of sinning. Yet my heart was calm. I knew what I was doing was from God. He would be responsible and would bring the matter to a good conclusion.

The next morning the Lord reaffirmed His will for my life: "I used suffering and sorrow to sanctify you. Now I will grant you grace and honor. My time has come; you can go." This was great news!

Shortly thereafter, someone knocked on my door and handed me a letter. If was from the other missionary. She congratulated me for turning defeat into victory, for being flexible. She wished me a bright future and great success.

That day was Saturday, and the workload was light. My friend Lien-Fang called at 9:00 a.m. and invited me for lunch. When we met she said, "Sister, I knew of your calling last year, and I deeply admire you. I want to help you financially. The Lord has led me to give you 1,000 silver dollars!"

As we talked at lunch, I told her, her mother and their friend, Miss Wei, principal of another school, about what God wanted me to do. They were excited and asked what they could do to help me. "I wish someone could refer me to a school in the United States," I told them.

"I will help you find a school," Principal Wei said. When she returned to her school, she immediately wrote a reference letter and mailed it. This was certainly beyond my expectations, but it strengthened my faith for what was ahead.

My heart was filled with joy when I returned to my room, but I did not express it outwardly. No one aside from the other missionary knew anything. Since Principal Tai had not granted her permission, I was still worried. Again I prayed, and as Gideon did, I came to the Lord three times and asked, "Lord, please allow me one more sign. If this is Your will then put these two words in Principal Tai's mouth: "a change."

Two days later Principal Tai greeted me in one of the classrooms. The first words she said were, "Do you want a change?" When I heard that all my fears departed, and I replied, "I want a change, but there are a lot of things involved in a change." So we sat down to talk. After she heard all that I had to say, she smiled and told me that she had discussed my situation with the assistant principal. They felt that the best thing for me to do was go abroad.

My heart soared at these words. The Sovereign Lord is great indeed! He is completely dependable. What He says, He means, and He never changes.

I went to the American Consulate office the next day to apply for a visa. Then I left for Chiang In to lead 10 days of revival meetings. God brought to pass the "change" that I desired in my heart.

7

God's Ambassador

Principal Tai arranged a farewell dinner in my behalf. At that dinner I was asked to give testimony of God's leading. I spoke of how the Heavenly Father loved me and sought me out at the age of nine. Many cried when they heard me tell of how my father sacrificed his life for me. Afterward, many of the students told me, "Why did you not tell us earlier of your experiences!"

So we would remember one another, a photographer took pictures. The students lined up and sang the "farewell" song, then they accompanied me to the pier. Amid tears, I boarded the ship "President Lincoln" and left Shanghai.

Missionary Peck traveled with me, and after 10 days at sea we reached San Francisco. That night we stayed at a hospitality house for missionaries, and I had the opportunity to witness and preach—without an interpreter!

Early the next morning, I boarded a train headed for Pennsylvania. After four long days, I finally arrived in DuBois and was greeted by Dr. and Mrs. An Moy. The next day was Sunday, and I was invited to speak at the Moy's church for the Sunday evening service. From that time on I had invitations to preach every Sunday—something totally unexpected.

At that time it took about two months for mail to travel from China to America, and because of that the school I was supposed to attend did not know when I was arriving. They wrote to Missionary Wei, thinking that I was still in China. They thought I could not make it for the spring semester and suggested I wait until fall. But when they found out I was in the States, they arranged everything for me to start school.

I kept busy every morning with my studies, which included preparing my sermons and typing them in English. I typed my sermons so I could keep them for the future. I studied theology and philosophy at the school during the day. And in the evenings, preached in different churches.

The Lord blessed my words. My meetings usually were packed, and some were turned away because there were not enough seats. Some people did not come because of the preaching, but because they had heard or read in the newspaper that I was from China and that I would be speaking on a certain day at a certain place. They came out of curiosity. But in the end they were attracted by the great power of the cross, and they could not resist coming back. The word spread of "this Chinese woman," and I had difficulty keeping up with the many invitations to preach.

One Sunday morning I was invited to speak at a Presbyterian church. I spoke from Isaiah 30:21, "Whether you turn to the right or to the left, your ears will hear a voice behind you, saying, 'This is the way; walk in it.'" Though I had only time to elaborate on my main points, the Lord was able to use the sermon. When I sat down, the pastor stood up and with tears in his eyes asked me to continue. "I have been a pastor and preached for many years," he said. "But I have never had the experience of communion with God's Spirit." At other services, pastors often would say, "We have sent missionaries to China to preach. God has sent you back to preach to us."

First day of school

I was warmly welcomed by everyone on the first day of school. Although I was the only Chinese student, the students were not biased in their attitudes toward me. Rather, they were kind, and they made me feel at home.

Not long after school began, a classmate named Ruth came to speak with me. I could tell she was in distress, and immediately she began to cry. She shared about something bad that had happened to her, and she hoped that I could give her some advice.

At first I did not know what to say. After all, I was from another culture. And though I had preached for a number of years and had counseled a number of people one to one, I had never been faced with a problem like Ruth's. But she was desperate for help.

So we knelt in prayer, and I called out to God as David did in Psalm 121: "I lift up my eyes to the hills—/where does my help come from?/ My help comes from the LORD,/ the Maker of heaven and earth." And He answered. From that time on Ruth's spirit was free. She understood the mystery of spiritual warfare. After this, the two of us often spent time together in prayer.

Ruth was just one of many who came for counseling. On Friday nights many would gather in my room to talk and pray. Sometimes we stayed up until the early morning hours. Most were eager to know how to lead a victorious Christian life—something the Lord had taught me through my past struggles.

The school was in the middle of New York City, and things there were very expensive. Through the referral of Missionary Wei, I received a scholarship. All those who received scholarships were required to work at the school. Some helped out in the library or kitchen, but I was asked to preach. I thank God for this because it gave me an unlimited number of opportunities to preach His good news.

Receiving the Lord's commission

One day as I was reading a news magazine, I came across an article about a famine in northern China. It told of families that had been separated from one another and children who were dying of starvation. As I read, I cried. I wished that I could have been transformed into a bird, so that I could fly to that place and do something to help my countrymen who were suffering.

Suddenly, I heard the Lord's voice speaking in my heart: "The people in the world are searching for love. There are three kinds of people in China today who have urgent needs: orphans, widows and the elderly who do not have children. Would you be willing to sacrifice yourself to go and love these people?"

"Lord, You know I have only one desire: to obey Your will, to let the people in the world know the wonderful saving grace of Your cross, to let them know that You are their Savior."

I prayed until about 2:00 o'clock in the morning. When I got up to prepare for bed, I noticed that the light was on in my friend's room across the hall. I gently knocked on her door, and she invited me in. I told her of God's call on my life and of my time of prayer. Suddenly, I recalled a dream I had years ago. In it, I had seen countless Chinese struggling in a river. Each was crying, "Save me! Save me!" As I ran by the shore, they extended their hands to me for help. I longed to help them, but my good intentions were not enough. I could not reach them all, and there was no one else to help. Then I heard the crack of guns going off and the sound of war. Somewhere, a battle had began. Then I woke up.

My friend was fascinated by the dream, and the two of us

wept and knelt down to pray, asking God to bring to fulfillment this great task He had committed to me. When I returned to my room, I offered God all the money I had—$2. This would serve as the initial funding for my future ministry among orphans and the elderly when I returned to China.

As the days passed, God confirmed His calling. After one service, two people came to me and said, "We know that when you return to China, God will use you to establish either a Bible school or an orphanage to train people to serve Him."

"Who told you this?" I asked cautiously.

"The Lord!"

Then I told them of my call. "There is a clear basis for your calling," they said. "God has given you many opportunities to preach. Why not mention this matter to the people you speak to? Perhaps that would be how He intends for you to fund your ministry in China."

I did not quite agree with this suggestion because I was trusting completely on the Lord. I was not willing to use my preaching to raise funds for my future ministry. When I told them this, they agreed and gave me their blessings. "Focus your heart on trusting the Lord," they said, "and you will have no anxiety. Because God has fulfilled His initial promise, He will bring into fulfillment what He has committed to you. We hope that after you return to China, we will receive news about the opening of an orphanage!"

From then on, I had no doubts about this revelation. And though I did not mention the need, I received funds from people who were moved by my preaching or testimony. They told me to use the money as I saw fit.

Preaching tour

That first school year flowed by as a swift river. Summer came, and my classmates were all getting ready to go home for the summer vacation. I, however, was busy responding to all those who had invited me to speak. My calendar was filled with engagements from all over the country.

At a Baptist church in Davenport, Iowa, a number of the people gathered with me early each morning to pray for the meetings and for missionary work in China. As we prayed, I could not keep from crying, thinking about those who were suffering. The Lord gave me this promise: "I have heard your prayer and seen your tears" (2 Kings 20:5).

The most unforgettable experience of that summer was when I was invited to speak at Faith Church. God worked in special ways. One woman testified, "A tumor had grown on the right side of my neck. It was as big as a bowl, and the pain was unbearable. After prayer I felt a gentle hand softly brushing across the tumor. Instantly, I felt something falling off my neck. I was immediately relieved and comfortable. It turned out that the tumor has disappeared without a trace."

That night as I preached, I felt a spiritual power upholding me. The Lord gave me a sermon entitled "Christians Should Represent Christ." As he closed the service, the pastor said, "I have never before heard such preaching."

Faith was the foundation of that church. They had gone through a number of trials and hardships before they were able to establish a church strong in faith. And so they called it the Faith Church. Right then I decided that the work that I would undertake when I returned to China must be founded on faith.

I preached at Chicago's Moody Church. Then I preached in a Christian and Missionary Alliance Church. God richly blessed that summer.

Receiving the whole blessing of the Lord

The busy summer vacation was over, but I still received letters inviting me to speak. One of my friends told me, "You are an ambassador sent by God to preach the saving grace of Christ. But more than that, because of God's power flowing through you, Christians have a changed perspective on life. Their lifestyles indicate significant changes. I hope that you can stay here in America to continue your ministry."

Someone else encouraged me to seek American citizenship. But God held His pillar of fire out before me, directing me back to China. I was still consumed by the passion to begin a ministry among the orphans, widows and elderly, though I had no idea how it would become reality. On the one hand, when I thought about this ministry, it was hard for me not to tremble with fear. But on the other hand, I had a great comfort for I knew that God is faithful and dependable.

Then one day a small voice spoke to me, "He will not withhold anything from those whose way of life is righteous." As I thought on this, other Scripture portions came to mind: "For in Christ all the fullness of the Deity lives in bodily form" (Colossians 2:9). "You may ask me for anything in my name, and I will do it" (John 14:14). How precious are those words! A person who belongs to God receives such powerful promises. If he has the faith to appropriate all these promises in his life, then he will not have to worry about anything he encounters. The phrase, "all the fullness of the Deity" includes knowledge, wisdom, talent, power, peace, joy, health, clothing, food, housing—everything! Again, I knew God was working out the details.

Leaving America for Europe

One afternoon, Missionary Foo came to see me at school. She was on furlough from China and had traveled to New York to visit some friends. She learned that I would be returning to China by way of Europe, so she invited me to visit her in

Wales, Great Britain. I happily accepted her offer. Not only did she suggest that I stop in England, but she also said that I should travel via Israel, where Christ was born and lived. I thought this would be a good opportunity to visit the Holy Land, so I applied for a visa and was accepted.

Many people came to see me off as I boarded the ship heading to England. I reached London after a week and took a train to Scotland. I visited a seminary there and was invited to share the amazing things that God had led me to do. One person there knew I was going on to Israel and wrote a letter of reference for me to her friend who allowed missionaries to stay with her. Again, the Lord answered prayer.

From Scotland I traveled to Wales and visited my missionary friend. I spoke in her church and visited a few schools. After a few days I returned to London and stayed at the YWCA. One day in the dining hall while I was having breakfast, I met a British woman. She heard that I was going to Jerusalem. "I have a cousin who works as head nurse at a hospital at Nazareth," she said. "I hope you can visit her. I will give you a letter of introduction."

A month later I left England, sailing for Israel. On the way the boat stopped in Marseilles, France, for one night. I toured the city with some of the other passengers, and after returning to the ship, a young woman from Russia, another one of the passengers, spoke to me.

She said that when she first saw me, she was moved in her heart to tell me her problems, hoping that I could help her. We talked and I explained the plan of salvation to her, stressing that God was able to handle any problem. She accepted the Lord and was instantly at peace.

Not long after this, another passenger approached me, a British man. He told of a difficult problem he was trying to resolve. Again, God gave me the opportunity to minister to him. After this man shared his concerns, I encouraged him to trust in God for help. In the end he agreed that this was the only way, and he asked me to pray for him.

We left Marseilles and crossed the Mediterranean Sea to Port Said in Egypt. After spending a night there, we proceeded through the Suez Canal. From there I took a train to Jerusalem.

8

War Comes and the Orphanage Opens

My tour of the Holy Land was a moving experience. At Bethlehem there is a chapel built on the site of Christ's birth. Close by is a mock-up of the stable where Mary gave birth to Jesus. As I thought of how the Son of God was willing to be born in a filthy manger, my heart broke. *Why do we shy away when we see poor people?* I asked myself. *Why do we not show compassion to them?* I knew the Lord was working in my heart, strengthening my resolve to return to begin His work.

Leaving Bethlehem, we traveled to the Garden of Gethsemane. Inside the Catholic church built on this site is a painting of the Lord Jesus kneeling with clasped hands and praying to the Heavenly Father. Close by hangs a painting depicting Judas leading a group of soldiers with torches, clubs, spears and swords to take the innocent Jesus. Again my heart broke with pain. I wanted to kneel down and cry. With tears I said, "Oh, dear Savior, You know my heart's desire is to follow You. Help me to be true until I have fulfilled the mission You have committed to me."

We visited other shrines and places where Christ is said to have done this or that. At the spot where Pilate's court was held, there were paintings of Jesus wearing a crown of thorns and a purple robe. One showed Him kneeling before the court with blood covering His face and body. Pilate was standing near a table and pointing his finger at the wounded Jesus. His eyes were peering into the crowd as if to say, "Look at this Jesus whose body is full of wounds. I find no fault in Him!"

I sighed inwardly. How strange that this sinless Jesus should suffer such pain for worthless humanity. There were five other people standing with me viewing this painting. We all knelt and worshiped the Christ who redeemed and sacrificed Himself for mankind. I saw more clearly than ever before the slain Savior who suffered for me. I wept and did not want to leave the place.

Finally, I reached Nazareth, and my English friend's sister. She opened her home and heart to me. After supper that first night, I had the opportunity to speak to the nurses at the hospital. Though they were from many different countries, we had one thing in common—a faith in God and His loving Son.

Invitation to India

While at Nazareth, I received an express letter one day from India. It was from a British missionary who worked with me in Shanghai. She wanted me to come to India. So after a month of touring Palestine, I departed from Israel and sailed through the Red Sea to Colombo, Ceylon, and northward to Manard Bay. From there, I took the train to Madras, India. Missionary Pai was waiting for me when I arrived at the train station.

The next day we took the train north to Niegiris. We visited a few church-sponsored schools, and I spoke several times. Due to the hot weather and the rough trip, I became sick. Resting in bed one night, I received a clear indication from the Lord that I would return to China that year and begin the orphanage. So even before I returned to China, I had a good idea when to start the work.

When Missionary Pai learned of my desire to begin a work to the needy, she expressed interest in helping me. Humanly speaking, this seemed as if it was a good idea. However, the Lord gave me two conditions to keep in my mind: she had to be in good health (the reason she left China for India was because of her poor health) and she had to have her own financial support. As it worked out, she decided not to come. God foresaw everything, and her not coming with me proved to be to my benefit later on.

Return to China

I stayed in India for three weeks, then once again boarded a ship. It was early summer, 1937, and I was going home. In Shanghai I stayed temporarily at the Ai-Yo School. Principal Tai hosted a welcome party for me, inviting me to share about my experiences abroad. Although there were many things to talk about, I felt led to speak about what God had called me to do.

Everyone who heard was deeply moved and responded overwhelmingly. What moved me most was the prayer of Missionary Fu. She prayed that since God had called me to this ministry, He would be responsible—no matter what other people thought. Her words were reassuring, but even so, there were still some concerns. The funds that I had were not enough for a down payment on a house large enough to start the ministry, let alone cover other expenses.

My mind was continually occupied by matters relating to my future work. Sometimes I would burst out in tears and say to the Lord, "Oh, Lord, thank You for letting me go abroad to study, preach and witness for You. I need Your help now. In all these years, my friends have witnessed Your faithfulness to me. I know that You will never change. Please show me how I am going to carry out the heavy task You have committed to me."

I admit, there was weakness in my faith, and it was hard for me not to worry. I often felt that the responsibility of establishing an orphanage was too great. *Why not just open a non-profit school and preach the gospel to the students?* I wondered. *It would make no real difference and be much easier.*

With this in mind, I set out one day to look for a building. I found one that rented for $33 a month. Classes could be held in the downstairs room, which would double as a chapel on Sundays. The upstairs was suitable for living quarters. However, I did not feel comfortable leaving a deposit, especially before I had clear indication from the Lord. I said in my heart, "If this is the Father's will, then He will keep this building and not allow someone else to rent it. I would wait until August 15 before paying the deposit."

Little did I know—but God knew everything—that war was about to break out and that the building would be destroyed. Actually, rumors of war were spreading before August. Principal Tai and the other missionaries who were vacationing in Tsing Tao came back. Principal Tai said to me, "China and Japan will be at war soon, and we don't know how long it will last."

But I suppose I knew all along that the Lord did not want me to start just a school. It seemed as if He was saying, "Nonprofit school, nonprofit school, why don't you think of an orphanage? Is it you who will feed the children? Clothe them? House them? Or is it I, Jehovah God?" I knew that this was another admonition from the Lord, and I quickly knelt down and asked Him to forgive my unbelief. "Please give me another promise," I prayed. When I opened the Bible I saw, "God is not a man, that he should lie,/ nor a son of man, that he should change his mind" (Numbers 23:19).

War breaks out

Early on August 13, the sound of bombs and shelling woke up the city of Shanghai. I prayed, telling the Lord, "God, the war has begun, and everyone counseled me not to begin the work of an orphanage. People say that this war will drag on for a long time. What should I do now?"

While praying, I remembered the dream I had in 1931. *Perhaps this is the fulfillment of that dream,* I thought. And since this war probably will last awhile, then I should begin immediately to help my countrymen who will suffer hardships. God used His Word to comfort me: "He fulfills the desires of those who fear him;/ he hears their cry and saves them./ The LORD watches over all who love him" (Psalm 145:19–20). The Lord would protect me from harm and would bring into fulfillment what He committed to me.

The next day I planned to go home and visit some relatives, but when I came close to Eight Hill Bridge, I heard a loud blast. An enemy warplane had dropped a load of bombs in the middle of the city. Minutes later, I heard sirens wailing as the ambulances raced to assist the injured. The streets were littered with pieces of dismembered bodies. It was an unbearable sight. At that moment the Lord brought another passage of Scripture to me:

> In those days it was not safe to travel about, for all the inhabitants of the lands were in great turmoil. One nation was being crushed by another and one city by another, . . . But as for you, be strong and do not give up, for your work will be rewarded (2 Chronicles 15:5–7).

That fall many schools could not open because of the war. When friends heard that I was determined to start an orphanage, they were worried. Someone said, "The schools cannot open. How can you possibly start an orphanage at this time? Where will you get food to feed the children?"

All this person said was true—from a human perspective—but not from God's. The God who has everything can bring something out of nothing. Faith can move mountains or empty the oceans! What is impossible for men is possible for God, because all things are possible with God (Mark 10:27).

Receiving the orphans and widows

On the morning of September 10, I went to visit a former classmate. As I went, I recalled the prayer of Jesus in Hebrews 10: "I have come to do your will, O God" (verse 7). My friend asked me, "Under these circumstances, it looks as if you won't be able to proceed with your plans for an orphanage."

"I believe that it is exactly under these circumstances that my ministry is needed most," I replied.

"Where are you going to live?" she asked.

"I was thinking of renting a small room near the Steel Gate."

"My family has a room that is empty now," she said. "You are welcome to stay there if you want to."

"I could not have asked for more," I said, full of joy.

That day, I informed Principle Tai that I would be leaving and thanked her for allowing me to stay at the school. "I have to concentrate on my new work," I told her. That evening a few friends went with me to my new room. They brought along a bed and a few pieces of furniture. They were concerned that I would feel lonely, but when they left I happily yelled out, "Whether it is a small house or a large house, where Jesus is, there heaven is."

About this same time, I learned of a widowed mother with

two children. They had no place to live or food to eat. Hue Chung Girl's High School was closed temporarily because of the war, so I asked about renting a bedroom temporarily to house the woman and her children.

After I got them settled, I noticed that the children were restless. Because school was closed, they had nothing to do. *Maybe if I could open a small school,* I said to myself, *it might meet some of the immediate needs.* So I contacted another friend and asked if I could use her guest room as a classroom. She agreed, and I placed an order with a carpenter to make 20 tables and chairs.

On registration day, nearly 30 children showed up! Although we could get by with the chairs and tables I had, I knew we were going to need another teacher. Again the Lord spoke, "On the mountain of the LORD it will be provided" (Genesis 22:14). When I made the need known, I immediately had several volunteers.

And so on the morning of September 13—just three days after I had talked with my friend—Immanuel Orphanage officially began.

Immediately, God began to bring other people. The fourth person was a 17-year-old girl who had been on the streets for nine years. It is hard to describe her condition. It took us hours to clean her up and care for the sores on her body. I then gave her some of my clothes to wear. When she was dressed, she looked as if she was a new person. In fact, she was. She had also asked Jesus to come into her heart.

After this we took in six more children who desperately needed food, shelter and schooling—and the love of God. But He was not through. More and more children came to our door. One was a 13-year-old girl who had been mistreated by her stepmother. Though her body was small, we could see from her hands that she was used to doing rough chores.

She told us, "When the rest of family is asleep, I am still

grinding soybeans. Often I have to get up at 1:00 in the morning, so I can be ready to sell the soy milk in the early market. After this, I have to go back home and do the family cooking. In the afternoon, I wash clothes and clean my brothers' and sisters' shoes.

"My stepmother always yelled at me, saying, 'You are a lazy worm. You have no future. All you do is eat. You might as well be dead!' If something I did was not pleasing to her, she would give me a beating."

Though Immanuel Orphanage was small, it was already meeting needs, and the future looked bright.

Spared from disaster

Two days before the fall of Shanghai to Japan, South City was shelled heavily. Due to the danger, we temporarily suspended classes at our school. During this time I wrote to my friends telling them about the opening of Immanuel Orphanage. As I wrote, the noise from the bombs and shelling was loud and frightening. That night South City burned furiously. The whole sky was lit up. My room was as bright as day.

The shelling gave me opportunity to expand the orphanage's ministry. Near the school, one family vacated their house because of the shelling. The house was large, three times the size of the space we were renting from the school. So I asked the departing family if they would rent it to me, and they agreed. With people fleeing from the approaching Japanese army, we quickly filled the house up.

Every Friday was bath day at the orphanage. On one particular Friday, the student who was in charge of the water boiler turned up the heat of the boiler and filled it with coals. After breakfast she went to the shower room to see if the water was hot. She got within a short distance of the room and heard a strange noise. She became scared and yelled out, "Help!"

Just then a resident on the third floor came running down the stairs yelling, "The water upstairs is boiling hot. What's going on down here?"

My niece, Wan-Ying Wu, who was one of my helpers, saw this excitement, and she rushed across the exercise field and into the dining hall, exclaiming, "Aunt, come quickly! A fire has started!"

I jumped up and ran to the shower room. All the students had fled. The Lord gave me the courage to go into where the boiler was. There was no fire—yet. The boiler was simply low on water. Were it not for the protection of the Lord, though, it could have turned into a big disaster. A week later we read in the newspaper of two houses where the water boiler exploded. A number of people were killed and injured, and the damage to buildings was costly. If the Lord had not extended His gracious hand to help, the work of Immanuel Orphanage would have been over.

9

The Work Expands but Encounters Some Problems

Four months after the opening of the Immanuel Orphanage, God told me that I should start a Bible class, so that those interested in studying the Bible would have the opportunity for further study. Three days later, a woman whom I had never met came to see me and asked, "Is this institution going to start a biblical studies class?"

"How did you know about this?" I asked incredulously.

"My name is Su-Chuen Wu," she said. "I've worked for a number of years at the TungTeh Maternity Hospital as a nurse. I also worked for Dr. King for several years. I received God's call last year directing me to preach in the outlying villages, but I felt that my knowledge of the Bible was insufficient. I've asked everywhere about a Bible school, but all of them have closed because of the war. It was not until today that I learned from friends that Immanuel Orphanage was planning on adding a Bible class. So I've come here to ask if you will accept me as the first student."

Listening to her, I thought that maybe God heard her prayers and inspired me to start the class. God had said to me, "Train up people to serve the Lord." Before I went to America to study, I was hoping to establish a Bible school in China. But because God had given me the burden to start the orphanage, I had no time to think about a Bible school. Now, I readily agreed to teach her.

In the spring of 1938, a mother and daughter came to the Bible class. She told me her story: "My name is Li-Wei, and I have two daughters. My husband is an alcoholic. I used to worry all day long, and I suffered from insomnia. After some time, my insomnia became so bad that I could hardly sleep at night, which left me groggy during the day.

"Then I started having strange dreams. One night I dreamed that two demons came and said, 'Time has come. Follow us, and we will take you up to the sky.' I quickly got out of bed and followed them to the living room, where they proceeded to teach me how to fly.

"When my family members discovered me, I was prostrate on the ground with my two arms flapping in a flying motion. They helped me back to bed, but as soon as I fell sleep, I had another dream. This time there were a number of demons, and I felt as if they were dragging me to the doors of death.

"Suddenly, an old man in white clothing appeared. After he hid me behind him, he knocked all the demons to the ground and said, 'She is mine. Do not harm her. I will use her in days to come to be my witness.' After I woke up, I felt at peace—and I had no more trouble with insomnia.

"At that time, I did not believe in Jesus. When I told my family about the dream, they agreed that the old man was Buddha.

"Later, I sent my daughters to boarding school, and I went to an adult school in Sung Chiang and completed the secondary courses after four years. About this time I started getting depressed again, and a relative came to see me and told me about your school. So I've come to study."

It is amazing how God uses different ways to lead people to Himself. This woman, Li-Wei, was not a Christian yet, but she had come seeking after truth. So we accepted her. Though she professed knowing about God and His Son Jesus on the first day of class, I knew she did not know anything about Christianity. When I spoke to her after class, she confessed that this was true. But she went on to tell me that the night before, she had a dream and saw Jesus speaking to her. He told her, "You must not doubt anymore. You must believe." As we continued to talk, she said that she wanted to accept Christ as her Savior, and we prayed.

Li-Wei's daughters also believed in the Lord, and He began to use her as a witness to others. After she finished studies at our Bible school, she went out to preach in the villages. Every time she came back to Shanghai to testify about how the Lord was working, everyone was moved to praise the Lord.

Relocation

As the work of the orphanage continued to expand, the number of students increased, and soon we ran out of room at the Wei-Chung Girl's High School. So we began to look for a new campus. Then in January 1939, I saw in the newspaper that some new buildings had just been constructed on Yu-Yuen Road. I did not know how much the monthly rent was, but God told me this was going to be the new home for our orphanage.

I immediately went to look at the place. As soon as I entered, I felt at peace. The ceilings were high, and the lighting was adequate. I felt as if I should kneel down and thank God right on the spot.

At first, I planned on renting two buildings, but each required an $880 deposit, and the monthly rent on each was

$215. This was much more than we could afford, so I ended up just renting one building. While I contacted the telephone and electric companies to connect their services, I sent the students to start cleaning the place.

The orphanage and school moved into the new facilities on February 2. People heard about our needs, and every day we received items such as lanterns, telephones, curtains, lamps and furniture. It was thrilling to see God work. All He had promised was coming to pass.

Disturbances from Satan

Most who came to the orphanage had never heard the gospel message and knew little about the Lord. But not long after they arrived, they turned their lives over to Jesus Christ. Then, thankful for what God had done for them, their life's aim became to serve Him and mankind.

But just when I thought things were going smoothly, I had a dream one night. I saw a lion standing behind me. His head was bowed and his mouth was wide open as if he were ready to swallow me. I yelled out, "The blood of Jesus is victorious!" I repeated it three times, and the lion disappeared. I said to myself in that dream, "I am like Daniel of ancient times who was protected by God in the lion's den."

After I woke up I thought it was just a bad dream and did not pay any attention to it. Little did I know that two weeks later, the orphanage was about to experience some unthinkable difficulties.

There was a student in the orphanage who was 20 years old, and one day she began acting strangely. At first she spoke about the Bible, encouraging people to repent. Then she began telling people their hidden secrets. At first we thought she was filled with the Holy Spirit. After all, what she said seemed logical. Then she came to me and said, "Jesus is discouraged! Immanuel Orphanage cannot continue to exist!"

A strange feeling passed over me, and I noticed her appearance seemed different. I told her, "Don't say foolish things. Jesus can never be discouraged!"

When she heard these words, it was as if someone had hit her. After a few minutes she said repeatedly, "Immanuel Orphanage will go through great tribulation." Each time she spoke, I calmly replied. "I am not afraid. With the Lord's presence I am not afraid."

Later that day, this student suddenly fell to ground and became rigid. She barely breathed. I picked her up and asked a helper to take her to my room. We prayed for her and sang a short chorus: "Defeat, defeat the old devil!/ With the cross of the Lord,/ defeat the old devil!" At this she cried out, "You cannot defeat me! My head is made of copper!"

The next morning I telephoned the missionary who had referred her to us. She was concerned and asked to see the student. My niece and I took her to the missionary. As we fasted and prayed together, the demon left her.

But Satan wasn't finished with us. A few days after the situation with the demon-possessed student, the orphanage suddenly was filled with a hazy smoke. A nasty smell permeated the air, and the food that was being prepared in the kitchen turned foul smelling. Then in the middle of the night, everyone was awakened by a howling noise.

The next day at noon, we held a special prayer meeting. As we prayed someone said she saw a giant black shadow pass through the wall. Immediately, the air cleared and a sense of peace returned.

It was during this time that I, too, felt oppressed. Those who felt that the orphanage was a bad idea thought that I would not be able to succeed without the help of Westerners. But the Lord was proving them wrong. We had no money, no supporters and no board of directors. All we could do was rely on God. Of course, that was the most we could do.

A year into our existence, we already had gained attention because of our success. God used fellow believers to help, pray and give. Then there were those of Shanghai's wealthier community who came to visit. They were pleased that the orphanage was something established by a Chinese person. They saw that the results were exceptional and were willing to donate money.

But still, after my dream about the lion, I felt that someone wanted to destroy the work of the orphanage for some unknown reason. I went to the Lord in prayer, and He gave me these comforting words:

> So do not fear, for I am with you;/ do not be dismayed, for I am your God./ I will strengthen you and help you;/ I will uphold you with my righteous right hand (Isaiah 41:10).

Relying on the precious promises God had given me, I bravely pressed forward. I knew the evil schemes of the enemy.

10

Five Days Under Japanese Siege

During the Sino-Japanese war, curfew was a common occurrence. The Japanese had taken control of Shanghai, and they decided the fate of the city.

I was out one afternoon on my way to visit a friend. Suddenly, however, I felt that I should return to the orphanage. As soon as I entered the alley that led to our building, a group of Japanese soldiers arrived and barricaded off the entrance. Evidently, someone had killed a Japanese there, and no one was allowed to enter or leave the area until the killer was apprehended. Nine out of 10 households in the area had family members away from home at that time, and they were not permitted to return home. But because of the Lord's prompting, I was able to return just before the blockade was erected.

Because we were not allowed to leave, obtaining food became a problem. When the barricade went up, we had just enough food for one day. Amazingly, a man from an outlying village had been in our area selling taros (a plant with an edible, starchy, tuberous rootstock). He needed to leave, but he could not sneak out with the taros. We met him just as he was pondering this problem, and we immediately purchased his load of taros to supplement our food supply.

The day before the blockade, the cook had purchased 50 pounds of vegetables for the next day's meal. But, for some reason, he broke his usual pattern of purchasing and went out on the day of the blockade and bought other food supplies. So now we had enough food to last for several days.

Then, on the afternoon of the third day, the tightly guarded gate was suddenly left half open. We quickly took advantage of the situation and bought a load of rice. As soon as the buyer crossed the gate back out of the alley, the soldiers suddenly appeared and the gate was closed once more.

On the morning of the fifth day, someone told me, "Miss Wu, we believe that the blockade will be lifted. We hear the prayers from the orphanage at four or five o'clock every morning, and we know that God will listen to such earnest pleading!"

That afternoon two friends tried to bring us some salted fish, radishes and other food items. At first the guards refused them entrance. Then as they turned to leave, they heard someone shout, "The barbed wire is open! Come back!"

Amazingly, our daily schedule through this five-day blockade went uninterrupted. I was not anxious the first four days, but on the afternoon of the fifth day, my heart was burdened. How would we solve this problem? I told the Lord, "There are many people here who belong to You, Father. Our food supply will be gone by tomorrow. If the blockade is not lifted, how are we going to survive? Please manifest Your great power and quickly deliver us from this grave problem!" In less than two hours, He answered.

The sick are healed

The Japanese were not the only problem we had to contend with. Because we were a large community, it was hard to avoid illness. But God was our Great Physician, and He answered our prayers for healing.

For example, one July night in 1939, a child woke up with a stomachache. She began to vomit and also had diarrhea. Then a number of other children experienced the same problems. Temperatures ran as high as 104.5 degrees. I gathered my helpers and the other children around, and we prayed for those who were sick. This message came from the Lord: "Have no fear of sudden disaster" (Proverbs 3:25.) Twenty-six people were sick, but in two or three days everyone was well!

On another occasion, a frail-bodied seven-year-old suddenly began to cough and had a rising body temperature. We rushed her to the hospital, and X-rays revealed that she had tuberculosis. The hospital refused to admit her for treatment. The orphanage had too many people, and it was hard for us to find a place to quarantine her. What would we do?

The whole orphanage prayed for her. Two weeks later, her fever suddenly receded, and she stopped coughing. The doctors thought we were foolish for bringing her back for another examination. But when they took another X-ray, they found that the area of her lungs that had been affected was healed.

Later, another girl contracted typhoid fever. She was only six years old, but I hesitated to leave her in the hospital by herself. So I took her to my room. A helper and I took turns looking after her for six weeks. On Sunday of the seventh week, the child told me that though she still had a fever, she believed that Jesus would heal her. She asked me to allow her to go downstairs to join the worship service.

It was unusual to see such strong faith in a child of her age, and so I carried her downstairs and placed her in a reclining chair. Before I preached, she stood up and said, "I want to praise Jesus. He healed my sickness. Were it not for

God's grace, I may have been dead by now. I wanted to come downstairs today to worship." During my sermon, I asked her two or three times if she was tired and wanted to go upstairs to rest. Each time she said no. The worship service lasted two hours, and when it was over we took her temperature. It had returned to normal!

One evening one widow experienced severe diarrhea. The next day it got worse, and she lost consciousness. In this frightening situation, the Lord gave me direction: "Do not panic, just pray for her. The Almighty God can heal her." So I requested a number of staff members to kneel beside her bed and pray with me for her, while the students gathered in the dining hall and prayed. It sounds unbelievable, but at the end of the prayer session, we immediately witnessed the result. In less than two days, her health was completely restored.

Expanding the orphanage

In December 1941, news reached us that Japan and the United States were at war. All the charitable organizations that received money from America were affected, and they had to cut back their services. As a result, the number of poor and dependent children looking for assistance increased overnight.

Late one night, I was unable to take in some new orphans because our building was overcrowded. Heartbroken, I turned to Lamentations and read, "Lift up your hands to him/ for the lives of your children/ who faint from hunger/ at the head of every street" (2:19). Next, I read Isaiah 54:2: "Enlarge the place of your tent, . . . lengthen your cords." As I read these words, it seemed that the Lord was going to expand Immanuel's facilities.

A few days later, a friend came to see me and said someone wanted to provide the expenses for an additional 50 orphans. I went right away and looked into renting the basement of the building next to us. It could house 40 or 50 persons.

The new orphans we took in were all malnourished. Two in particular were in pitiful condition. Their skinny bodies were covered with boils. I immediately gave them haircuts, baths and washed and repaired their clothes. And we started them in school.

In two years' time, these illiterate children were able to write short letters. Here is the testimony one of them wrote:

> I used to live in the home of my uncle, but he mistreated me. He sent me to work in the fields every day. One day I became too tired to do any more work. When my uncle saw that I had stopped working, he gave me a beating. After this, I ran away to Shanghai. I had no place to go and so I ended up begging on the streets. While I was on the street, someone saw me and brought me to Immanuel Orphanage. I was able to eat, go to school and learn about Jesus.

Lonely widows

One day the former principal of Wei-Ling Girl's High School in Su Chou came to see me. As we talked she told me, "There is a former student of Wei-Ling who is in a difficult situation. Her parents are dead, and her husband has left her for another woman. A few months ago she became sick and almost died. She is still in the hospital, but the doctors said she has to leave. Do you think you can help her?" I was touched by the woman's situation and immediately agreed to take her in.

Three days later she brought the woman to the orphanage. I was busy when they arrived, so I sent a staff member to greet them. The staff member looked at her and wondered how could such a weak person survive. But in a short time her health began to improve, and she was even able to help out in the kitchen.

When I had opportunity to speak with her, she told me her life story. Not long after she finished school, her father died and her relatives forced her to marry. When war broke out she and her husband fled to Su Chou and stayed with her mother. Sometime later her husband went to Shanghai on business and did not return.

Finally, the woman and her mother traveled to Shanghai to search for the missing husband. They found that he was fine, that he set up a business and that he had three mistresses!

The woman divorced him, but she and her mother were left with no source of income. A short time later, the mother died. After all she had gone through, the woman broke down, mentally and physically. Principal Lan heard about her illness and arranged to have her put in the hospital, where she stayed for three months. Gradually, her condition improved. But when it came time to leave the hospital, there was no place for her to go.

That same day, I had the opportunity to lead her to Christ. How she praised God for what He had done for her!

Though we had taken in other widows, the Lord reminded me anew that this was an important part of the ministry. And as the weeks and months passed, it seemed as if more and more were coming to our door. One day an elderly blind woman appeared. Her husband had died young, and they had no children. Her livelihood depended on her sewing. But after 37 years, her eyes began to deteriorate, and she could no longer thread a needle. She could only use what was left of her savings and loan it out to earn a little interest to provide for her old age.

Then the war started and everything in her house was destroyed. Someone took all her savings and fled. Soon afterward, she went completely blind. She went to stay with her brother but could not get along with her sister-in-law and had to leave. Faced with complete poverty, she recalled from her youth hearing about Jesus. Though she did not accept Him then, she was impressed with what she heard. Now she was in trouble and had no place to go for help, so she cried out to God. Soon He directed her to our institution.

Not long after this woman arrived, I received a call asking me to take in another widow, who was 88 years old. Her son and daughter-in-law were both dead. Due to her advanced age, I did not want to take her in. Later, however, God spoke to me about her: "She is very old and will not have many days here on earth. If she comes to the orphanage now she can have the opportunity to hear the gospel and be saved." I then telephoned my friend and told her I would take the woman in.

Soon after she arrived, she said to me with tears in her eyes, "I have had a hard life. While at home I used to be scolded for no reason at all by my daughter-in-law and my grandchildren. I did not have enough to eat nor was I able to sleep. My heart was troubled and worried. I was like someone drowning, an old woman waiting for death. I was fortunate that you were moved by God's love to take me in. Now I can sleep at night. I cannot find words to express my appreciation."

Extension in Chin-Ru

As the war continued, so did the stream of children and others looking for a home. We again found ourselves at capacity level and needing to expand. We began using the dining hall as classroom space, and at night we had to put tables together to make beds.

Again, I went before the Lord with our need. In my personal devotions, I told Him, "You have been faithful in everything. I have always been dependent on You. Please help us

acquire a building that can be used to expand the orphanage."
The Lord gave me an answer from Job: "He is wooing you from
the jaws of distress/ to a spacious place free from restriction"
(36:16).

A half hour after my devotions, a friend came to visit. She
told me, "There is a school residential hall on the west side of
Chin-Ru available for rent. Although it has only one floor, it is
big. There are plenty of windows, and there is a large yard. The
school is empty. What do you think?"

"I think the Lord has answered our prayers!" I said.

We contacted the caretaker and arranged to rent the
building. I took the staff and students to clean up the place,
and in three days it was ready to be occupied. More than 70
people were moved to the new building.

On the first day, some friends of the orphanage came to
inspect the place. Moved by what they saw, they contributed several thousand dollars to cover the first month's rent, moving
expenses and the purchase of rice.

After the extension facility opened, we took in an additional 50 orphaned children. Each one, it seemed, had a
hardship story. One girl's parents gave her away to another
family as their future daughter-in-law. She told me, "I was
young and did not understand what was happening. I was
often beaten and yelled at. My new parents were troubled
with money problems, and they took it out on me. On numerous occasions, they beat me until I lost consciousness.

"The neighbors learned of their abuse and took me into
their home and hid me. But my foster mother found out and
took me back. When she got me home, she gave me an even
worse beating.

"Finally, a neighbor asked you if I could come to the
orphanage, and, thankfully, you agreed. In my 13 years of
life, this is the first time I have experienced the love of a
mother."

Another teen, a 14-year-old girl, had an even worse story. Her birth mother had died, and she and her younger brother had been placed with foster parents. In a fit of rage the foster mother took a piece of glass and cut the girl's foot, causing it to become infected. Another time, she went berserk and strangled the brother to death. Then she asked the girl to go out to the field in the middle of the night and bury his corpse.

A few months later on a bitter cold morning, the girl woke up to find no one at home. The door to her room was locked, and she could not get out. Finally, the neighbors heard her yelling and freed her. There was no food left in the house, so the only thing she could do was to beg on the streets. She was miserably cold and hungry and eventually fell sick.

Fortunately, an American missionary came by and took pity on her. He took her to a hospital and paid for the doctors to care for her. Three months later, she came to Immanuel Orphanage. "Words cannot tell of the abundant grace of Jesus!" she told me.

11

Relying on
Almighty God

When I first began the orphanage, the income was just enough for us to break even. To set aside a sum for an offering was difficult. On one occasion in 1937, I prayed, "God, please give us Your blessings this month. Heap grace upon grace so that the money we receive will give us a surplus after we pay all the expenses. That way we will be able to give an offering."

God answered—abundantly! After paying all the expenses there was enough money left to meet the goal set for that year's offering.

One night, a Christian brother came and asked if we would take his daughter. He was having financial problems and was unable to feed her. We originally had set up our ministry as a place to help orphans and widows. Children who had both parents could not be admitted except under special circumstances. Just as I was thinking this, though, the Lord brought a passage of Scripture to my mind: "Suppose a brother or sister is without clothes and daily food. If one of you says to him, 'Go, I wish you well; keep warm and well fed,' but does nothing about his physical needs, what good is it?" (James 2:15–16).

Right at that moment, there was no money left in the

offering fund. But I could not disobey God's command to help a fellow Christian, so we took money from the orphanage's general funds and gave it to him.

The next morning God sent someone who gave us $5,000 in a savings bond. We set aside a sum for the offering fund and what was left made up what we had taken from the general fund.

On another occasion, a patron donated a $10,000 savings bond to the orphanage. We took out $1,000 and sent it to another mission agency. Later, when I visited them, the director was almost moved to tears. She told me, "Our balance sheet last month showed we were short $1,000, and we didn't know where we would obtain the money. Then your check arrived. We are thankful to God for His goodness."

Rice price skyrockets

In the winter of 1939 the price of rice suddenly jumped from $12 a bushel to $40. We were shocked when we heard the news. We had tried to be frugal in our expenditures, but now this situation arose. God used the situation, though, to make us depend on Him. During this time we continued serving three meals a day. The staple was flour and rice supplemented by squash, peanuts and yams.

Later, through a friend's help, the Red Cross donated 50 sacks of wheat to the orphanage. Then, through another friend, we were able to buy 10 bags of rice from a government agency. But within a few months, not only was it difficult to buy rice but also other foods. The war was causing a shortage. But God kept working in our behalf, moving fellow believers to donate 2,000 pounds of rice noodles to us.

Then one day, the merchant we purchased rice from told us that we could no longer pick up our whole order; it had to be given out in parcels. However, we needed all the rice to feed the children. So my niece, Ching-Ying, and another staff member went to the man to see if he would give us the full order.

The merchant said, "No, we cannot do it. The government has imposed sanctions. This morning a number of merchants have already encountered problems, and their shops were almost closed down because of it. Government inspectors are watching the shops closely."

As he was speaking, Ching-Ying recalled a verse from Psalms: "The LORD's unfailing love/ surrounds the man who trusts in him" (32:10). She then told the man, "We believe in Jesus. He has supernatural powers that can protect us from harm. Please trust us. We will be responsible for ourselves and will not cause problems for your shop."

Finally, the clerk agreed. They loaded their cart with 2,000 pounds of rice. Outside, there were several police cars, but none of the officers said anything to my niece and her companion. At the checkpoint, the guard saw the cart go by. He stared but did not question them. A short time later, they arrived back at the orphanage, safe and sound!

Food becomes more scarce

Shanghai began a rationing system in early 1942. Coupons were given according to the number of people in a household. A special permit had to be acquired from the Bureau of Food if there were more than 30 people at one location. The orphanage was allocated seven bags of rice a month, which was only enough for nine days. Whatever we lacked we had to make up ourselves. Thank the Heavenly Father that He sent kind-hearted people who gave us oatmeal, flour and cornmeal.

But in March the next year, the government stopped the allocation of the seven bags of rice. Rice was becoming harder and harder to obtain, so the orphanage and the branch had to get by on supplemental food. Eventually, we had to purchase rice from Nan-Hsiang and ship it down to Shanghai. But this was a burdensome process. There were military checkpoints at every junction on the way.

On one occasion, Ching-Ying and a helper went to Nan-Hsiang to purchase wheat. On this day, the government officials ordered that no supplies could leave the city because all vehicles were needed elsewhere. Finally, at four o'clock in the afternoon, they saw five empty carts that had came from Shanghai loaded with telephone poles. They were preparing to return to Shanghai with no cargo, so they immediately agreed to transport the wheat.

At the mid-point in the journey, they met a cart coming toward them. The people in the cart told them to return to Nan-Hsiang. The bridge ahead was out, and a bus had fallen into the river. Ching-Ying decided to push on, however. They knew the orphanage needed the food.

When they reached the bridge, they saw that there were still two planks left to cross over on. So the men pulling the carts unloaded the sacks and carried them across by hand. Then they pulled the carts over. After a long trip, they finally made it to Shanghai.

Paradise in the midst of war

In 1944 a woman came to visit the orphanage. She knew me from the past, having heard me preach. After she toured the orphanage, she told me, "I think it would be a good idea if you wrote about your experiences of starting this place."

I had never thought of it before, but it sounded as if it was a good suggestion. We had many visitors, and they all wanted to know the details of our day-to-day operation as well as how the orphanage got started.

The woman said that if I wrote the story, she would pay

the entire cost of publishing the book. After prayer, I felt God's blessing, and I immediately began to write. But because I did not want to keep talking about myself, I left out some of the details.

When Ching-Ying looked at what I had written, she said, "Auntie, how can you write this way? The good stories have all been changed. Why don't you let me help with the writing?" I agreed.

After the final draft was finished, we had not yet thought of a suitable title. I asked the Lord what I should call it, and He said, "When did this orphanage begin?"

"In the midst of war," I answered. Just then the title came: *Paradise in the Midst of War.*

A new building

One day a friend from the neighborhood told us about a three-story apartment house at the entrance to our alley that was for sale. The asking price was $2.5 million in savings bonds (the Chinese dollar had been drastically devalued). Just before I found this out, I had learned that the Japanese army had been looking at the building in which we housed our branch in Chin-Ru. We knew that at any moment they could take it over for their own use, forcing us to leave.

So we committed the situation to the Lord, asking Him to provide another location for the branch. It would be ideal, we prayed, if the location was in Shanghai and in the same alley as the orphanage. Then we heard the news of the building for sale. The Heavenly Father had prepared a place that could house more than 100 people right in our own alley! However, the asking price was way beyond our means.

Our orphanage had never solicited money from people. Sometimes when we ran short of funds, our treasurer would go to the rice merchant or baker and ask for credit until the next day. And the Lord always provided the money for us to repay.

One time, the treasurer went to the fruit store and asked for $25 worth of credit. The owner wanted her to give him a check in return. Because all our transactions were in cash, we did not have a bank account.

The next morning, God sent a visitor who donated $25— by check. The treasurer took it to the market and bought the food we needed.

Though the sum for the building was great, we had a great God, and we knew that if He wanted us to have the property, He would provide the money. And as people learned of the situation, money began to pour in.

During the first few days, however, I did not have faith to believe that the sum could be raised, and I thought about using the ways of men to "help" God. My book *Paradise in the Midst of War* had been published, and I thought about asking the various schools in Shanghai to sell it and use the money toward the purchase of the building.

But God had other ideas. I woke up one morning with the Lord whispering in my ear, "If a father took his children on a trip, would he break his promise and abandon the children on the way?" I knew that my idea was wrong; God would deliver on His own time, in His own way—without my help.

The money continued to come until we only lacked $300,000. After the whole orphanage prayed one afternoon, suddenly, the door bell rang. One of the helpers went to answer it and was stunned to find a person with a check made out for just the sum we needed—$300,000! Now we could purchase the building, and the Chin-Ru branch could move to Shanghai.

At our New Year's Eve dinner, the last group of teachers and students finally arrived from the branch. On the second day after our evacuation, the Japanese army took over the

Chin-Ru building. What a miracle God had accomplished!

12

America Revisited

The war ended in August of 1945, and there were celebrations everywhere. On September 13, the Chinese government sent a representative to investigate our orphanage. He asked that we register with the government and explained that official certification would benefit the orphanage. For one thing, our food supply would be guaranteed. (However, we had our guarantee of a constant food supply—the Heavenly Father. During the eight years of war, none of our people went hungry.)

Registration with the government required that we form a board of directors, which we did. The registration process progressed smoothly, and when we received the certificate, the official in charge wrote the words "exceptional performance."

After the war, Western relief organizations sent supplies to China. We gratefully received what was given to us, but we felt we could not accept any monetary help. One group, for example, after their representatives visited us, promised to send $2 per person per month. By this time we had more than 300 people in our care, which qualified us for $600 a month or $7,200 a year. But I felt in my heart that the Lord did not want us to accept their offer.

Another group wanted to help us expand the orphanage. This, too, was an enticing offer, but again I had to turn it down. The Lord would not let me accept. Little did I know that in a short time, these decisions would be among the most important I ever made.

God heals me

Shortly after the war ended I received a letter from a former classmate in America suggesting that I come back to America for further studies. I was tempted to do so, but my responsibilities at the orphanage made it impossible for me to leave. But beyond that, my health was poor. I had labored long and hard at the orphanage during the war years, and the work had taken its toll on my body.

Late one night I began to vomit blood. I waited until daybreak before I sat up at the side of the bed. My niece and other helpers who slept in the next room came in to see me and saw that my complexion was pale. And they saw that the spittoon was half full of fresh blood. They were frightened and wanted to call the doctor immediately. I told them not to worry. "The doctor can cure people's sickness," I said, "but can he heal as quickly as Jesus?" I then instructed them not to mention my vomiting blood to any of the others.

After dinner that night my condition deteriorated, and I continued to vomit blood. Later, the teachers told the children of my illness, and the whole group gathered to pray for me.

I finally went to sleep, and while I slept I had the strangest dream. Everyone in the orphanage was dyeing eggs red. Each egg had these words written on it, "The Lord is risen. The Lord is victorious." After I woke up, I spoke to the student who was keeping me company for the night and told her about my dream. Then I told her, "The Lord Jesus was resurrected on the third day. I will be healed on the third day!"

The next day, a friend came to visit. When she learned that I was sick, she got down on her knees and prayed. Right then, God gave her two Bible verses for me: "He is not weak in dealing with you, but is powerful among you. For to be sure, he was crucified in weakness, yet he lives by God's power. Likewise, we are weak in him, yet by God's power we will live with him to serve you" (2 Corinthians 13:3–4). These words fit well with my dream. When Christ was nailed to the cross, those around Him thought it proved He was weak after all. But because of God's great power, Christ rose from the dead. My body also was weak, but if I relied on God's strength, my health would be restored.

Indeed, I was better on the third day. I got up from bed and said, "Because God has healed me, why should I live as a sick person?" And I carried out my regular duties with no further problems.

The missing key

The chores in the orphanage were divided among the children according to their age and strength. The older students were required to take cooking classes, and they took turns doing kitchen duties.

At 4:00 a.m. on my third day of illness, the student in charge of cooking the rice soup got up to go to the kitchen. When she reached for the key to the kitchen, which she left laying on the table beside her bed, it was not there. She looked everywhere but could not find it. Her partner was waiting for her, so she quickly got ready and went out.

Since they could not get in the kitchen, they thought they might as well sift the rice, which was in the storage room. They reached for the sifter, and to their surprise, the key fell out. One of them began sifting the rice, while the other went to the kitchen to start a fire to boil water. Because they wanted to be ready for the 7:00 a.m. breakfast time, she turned up the heat higher than usual so the soup would cook faster.

A few minutes later, the water boiler began to make strange noises. One of the girls ran to get the repair person. He came, examined the pipes and said in amazement, "God has His hand on this orphanage. The cold water pipe that runs into the boiler was closed. Without cold water coming into the boiler, it could have exploded!"

We do not how God caused the key to disappear, but it proved providential. Had the girls began cooking at the scheduled time, no doubt the boiler would have exploded. In my devotions I read, "No weapon forged against you will prevail" (Isaiah 54:17).

Traveling abroad

I fell sick again in 1946. The diagnosis revealed that I had a relapse of pneumonia. A nurse visited me twice a day and gave me medication. Two months later, though I was better, I felt very weak. It was during this time that I received a second letter from my friend in America. Again, she wanted me to come to the United States to study—and to rest.

The board of directors and supporters of the orphanage were in agreement that I should go abroad for a year of rest, and the arrangements were made. A few months later, in August, I left for America. I would receive financial support from the board, and Ching-Ying would take over the day-to-day responsibilities of running the orphanage.

My first night in America, the Lord revealed to me that I should translate my book and print it in English. The next day I went to see my alma mater in New York City. I was able to stay on campus and immediately began work translating *Paradise in the Midst of War*. When it was finished and printed, I sent copies of the English edition to my friends across America and around the world.

The dean of the school one day held up my book in front of those gathered for chapel and said, "This book is a blessing to people. I have read every word in it, and I hope that everyone in this seminary will have a chance to read it."

As copies of my book went out to different parts of the country, letters inviting me to speak began pouring in. Readers were touched by the amazing accounts of how God worked in my life.

One afternoon, an elderly woman came to the seminary to see me. She wanted me to come stay with her for a few days. I had just recovered from the flu and did not want to venture outside. But a week later, she sent a car for me. This time it was hard for me to turn her down, so I went to her house. I had never met her before, nor did I know how she knew about me.

When I arrived at her house, she told me, "I have received letters from my friends mentioning you and your ministry." Then she said something that shocked me: "You have a shortcoming."

"I do?" I asked, curious to hear what she would say.

"Yes. When you have a financial need, you never mention it to anybody."

I smiled when I heard this. "God wanted me to establish this ministry," I told her. "He is the Father of the orphanage, and He is ultimately responsible. The facts bear out His faithfulness. When the children, helpers or I ask for His help, He meets the need. I do not find it necessary to ask people for help."

She agreed with what I said, but she asked, "Aren't you afraid of what will happen in the future? Everything is going OK for now, but what if something happened to you?"

Without much thought I replied, "The only thing I am afraid of is losing my faith. If something happened to me, the Lord would see to it that someone else took over the orphanage."

As we continued to talk, she expressed concern over the fact that the orphanage did not have a regular source of income. She also mentioned that she had thought of establishing such a ministry herself, but she did not think she could find a suitable person to run it. At this, I understood why she had asked me to her house—to consider helping her start an orphanage. But I could not do what the Lord had not called me to. My work, I told her, was still in China.

Before I left America, the Lord enabled me to financially assist the school that had done so much for me. The seminary was located in New York City where the rent was high, and it was in debt.

I am glad that at the end of my first visit to America in 1937, I obeyed the Lord and returned to China. I could have stayed in the U.S. and no doubt had a successful preaching ministry. I could have obtained more schooling. But if I had not returned to my homeland, I would not have experienced the Lord's blessings, nor would I have been able to help those in need. The Lord Jesus said, "What good will it be for a man if he gains the whole world, yet forfeits his soul?" (Matthew 16:26).

13

Darkening Clouds

I returned from America to a new country—a Communist one! In my absence, Communists had overthrown the Chinese government. One night in the spring of 1954, I dreamed that I was on a journey. The road I traveled was rolling and uneven. The left and right sides were higher than the road itself, and it seemed as if I were walking down an alley. As I continued walking, I encountered fallen walls, piles of sand, mud, stones, wood and tree branches. After a while, it became almost impossible to walk, and at one point I fell down.

Then, suddenly, I found myself on a flat road. Walking beside me was my niece Ching-Ying. When we came to a side path, I told her, "Wait here. I am going to visit the person who lives in the house over there. I will be back shortly."

When I reached the house, I discovered an elderly woman. As we began to talk, I said to her, "I will no longer be in charge of Immanuel Orphanage. I am going to die soon." The woman wept at these words.

I returned to the road but did not see Ching-Ying. I called out to her, but there was no response. I was all alone on this wide road.

One thing that comforted me was the brilliance of the sun. I bathed in its warm glow as I continued my journey. At this point, I woke up. This was certainly a strange dream, and I could not imagine its meaning. But it would not be long until I found out.

The government assumed that because of my connection with Westerners, Immanuel Orphanage was receiving financial subsidy from abroad. For that reason, the officials wanted us to register with the new government—more so they could keep a close watch on our outside-of-China connections than because they were worried about rules. I appealed this requirement, stating that we did not have any regular financial help from foreigners.

Finally, the government relented and did not require us to register. But they did ask me to submit a regular report on the orphanage's actions. And the officials often sent someone by to inspect the orphanage. In addition, we were asked to send a representative to the meetings of the citywide orphanages. I also made sure to follow the government's requirements in teaching the children to be good citizens and to obey the rules and regulations of the government.

During this time, government officials praised our work. Every time inspectors came, they talked about the good we were accomplishing. They even spoke of how much the government's cadres could learn from us. Somehow, though, I suspected something was not quite right.

"A refuge in the day of disaster"

The day-to-day responsibilities of the orphanage kept me busy. Although I did not know what would happen each day, I relied on the Lord and calmly went through one day at a time. Jeremiah 17:16-17 says, "I have not run away from being your shepherd;/ you know I have not desired the day of despair./ What passes my lips is open before you./ Do not be a terror to me;/ you are my refuge in the day of disaster."

Then one day, a notice came from the government saying that in the future all orphanages would be run by the government. At that time all orphanages in the city except ours had already been taken over by the government, and some of the directors had been arrested and jailed.

My close friends began to urge me to give in, but I could not. This was God's orphanage, and from the beginning to now, He had been responsible for the work. I could not do anything—even if meant going to jail—without His leading. Beside, I dare not give these children over to the atheistic, Communist government.

In August we had a discipline problem with two of the older boys. They asked permission to go out one afternoon to meet a friend. As I questioned them about where they were going, I found out that they were going to meet some girls (who previously had been expelled from the orphanage) and go to a movie. Of course, when I discovered this, I refused their request and told them they would be punished for lying.

I used the occasion of a student assembly to bring up the matter, asking the other students to give their opinions on what should be done to the two. Before anyone could speak, though, the two boys stood up and, with tears in their eyes, admitted their wrong thinking. Three government cadres were present at that meeting.

This was the excuse the government had been waiting for. The next morning two policemen came to my door. They started by asking questions about my health, but a few minutes later, one of them produced a pair of handcuffs and said, "You are a counterrevolutionary and are under arrest." They handcuffed me and placed me in the back of their van. I was charged with the crime of "harboring the country's counter-revolutionaries"—the two boys who wanted to meet their girlfriends. Not long after I left, a car came with the orphanage's new director—a government official—and as quick as that I lost the orphanage.

At first, I was shocked and frightened. But the Lord brought peace and calm to my heart. I remembered a verse from John: "Peace I leave with you; my peace I give you. I do not give to you as the world gives. Do not let your hearts be troubled and do not be afraid" (14:27). I was His, and nothing could happen to me without His allowing it to happen. The peace in my heart was as stable and firm as a mountain.

That same afternoon, I was brought to trial. Without my knowing it, the police had rounded up the whole orphanage and took them to a meeting place. There they asked anyone who had knowledge of my wrongdoings to come forward and tell them. Five frightened, young students went up and made false accusations against me. They accused me of having ties to American imperialism. They said that I had a secret radio and was spying for other countries. They also told how I had been receiving money from the Kuomingtang Nationalistic Party and that I had forced some orphans to their death and others into mental institutions. All these statements, of course, were false.

But the government had what they wanted. The judge said, "In 17 years you have done many good things, but you also have committed many wrong acts." After naming all my alleged "crimes," he asked me to confess to them. Because they were not true, I refused. So I was placed in jail until evidence could be obtained of my guilt. But try as they might, the officials were unable to find any clear evidence that I had committed the crimes. They were not, however, going to let me out of jail.

An object of grace

Though I tried to remain joyful in jail, my health began to fail. One night, an officer was making his midnight rounds. He heard a noise coming from my cell and asked if I was crying.

"No," I said, "I am sick with a fever."

He then gave me a cup of water. As I thanked him, my heart welled up with praises and thanks to the Lord. He was fulfilling His promise:

> "When you pass through the waters,/ I will be with you;/ and when you pass through the rivers,/ they will not sweep over you./ When you walk through the fire,/ you will not be burned;/ the flames will not set you ablaze" (Isaiah 43:2).

I also remembered the story of Joseph from Genesis. God made him "an object of grace" in the eyes of those in charge of him: "the LORD was with him; he showed him kindness and granted him favor in the eyes of the prison warden" (Genesis 39:21).

That winter the weather was harsh, and the conditions at the camp were terrible, especially for someone like me who suffered from severe bronchitis. I was coughing continually and vomiting. Eventually, I lost my appetite.

One night I lost the feeling in the lower parts of my body. The next morning the officer in charge reported my condition to his superior, who ordered the guards to carry me to his office. The man told me, "We are going to let you leave. You need medical attention. Can you call someone to come for you?"

I immediately telephoned my brother, and he came for me. He took me to my nephew's home.

One week later I was rushed by ambulance to the Yi-Ho

Hospital, where they discovered that my blood pressure was severely elevated, which was causing the paralysis in my lower extremities. Also, a tumor had developed in my lungs and was infecting my lymph glands. And my bronchitis had deteriorated into asthma.

Who could prescribe medication for such serious illnesses that could produce instant results? The things that are impossible for men are possible with God. Up to this point in my life, I had many close calls with death. But Almighty God exercised His resurrection power and rescued me from the pit of death.

From man's point of view, I should have been dead by now. Someone even said to me while I was in the hospital, "You do not need to pray anymore. Your sickness has not been healed."

"I will be healed!" I replied.

According to the prognosis of my illness, my reply was a denial of facts. But it was because of God that I could give such a firm reply. "For he knows how we are formed,/ he remembers that we are dust" (Psalm 103:14).

Admittedly, because I was so sick, I did struggle with believing that God would heal me. I laid in bed all day, useless to men and to God. One day, as David did, I cried out to God, "O Lord, have mercy on me;/ heal me" (41:4). "Sustain me according to your promise, and I will live;/ do not let my hopes be dashed" (119:116).

Then, one night after dinner, I heard the still, small voice of God: "The end of winter is the beginning of spring." When I thought about the meaning of this, my heart was filled with joy. Here was a message from God that my health would improve. Just as the dead plants returned to life, so I would rise from my sick bed.

A month later, I was well enough to leave the hospital. When the government authorities heard this, they immediately sentenced me to five years confinement—to be served under house arrest.

A wonderful thing happens

When I left the hospital, I stayed temporarily in the house of my friend Kwei-Lien Fan. She was a nurse, and this was a good arrangement. She worked to help me overcome my paralysis, which was my primary health concern.

Time went by fast, and one morning, two months after I left the hospital, I was full of joy. Suddenly, I felt as if a heavy load had been lifted off me. My limbs were relaxed. I swung my legs off the bed and put my feet on the floor. Slowly, I rose to my feet and walked!

When my sister-in-law, who was visiting, saw me, she burst out laughing and clapped her hands. Kwei-Lien was in the kitchen when she heard the noise. She ran to the door and said: "What is causing the two of you to be so happy?"

"Come and see for yourself!" I shouted. "I can walk! My paralysis is healed! Glory be to the name of the Lord!"

On Wednesday and Saturday afternoons, my friend Li-Mei Tu came to visit me. Often she would prepare a meal of meat and fish that the food ration coupons allowed for. I was thankful for her care and concern. God foreknew what would happen to me, and He prepared Li-Mei to be my special helper. I was hoping that God would arrange it so that she and I could move into an apartment together.

One afternoon not long after this, Li-Mei came and said, "Dear teacher, I have good news for you. I believe the Lord wants us to get an apartment together. That way we can take care of each other."

"You did not mention this before you left last night," I told her.

"I know, but last night as I lay in bed, I suddenly heard the

Lord speak. Early this morning, I spoke to my landlord and told her why I needed to leave. She agreed."

Not long after, we found a nice place to live and moved in. As we worked arranging the furniture and unpacking, we sang a chorus from Zephaniah 3:17: "The LORD your God is with you,/ he is mighty to save./ He will take great delight in you,/ he will rejoice over you with singing." From that moment on, we relied on each other for many things, and we never had an argument or disagreement. Again, God had granted the desire of my heart.

Twice searched

One afternoon, government officials showed up at our door and said they wanted to search the apartment. They came in and began poking around in every crack and crevice. Li-Mei gathered all her valued possessions and laid them on a table. Then, after about two or three hours, they left.

However, a short time later, they showed up at the high school where Li-Mei was teaching. They took her out of class and brought her back to the house. They made her stand in the alley with her head bowed and her hands behind her back.

When I came out to see what was going on, one of them told me, "Bring out all your weapons." At first I thought of replying, "We don't have any weapons." But I had a second thought and went back into the house. I brought out the kitchen knives and a pair of scissors. Then I was made to stand behind Li-Mei while they conducted another search of our apartment. They looked everywhere but, of course, came up with nothing. I had no counterrevolutionary literature nor even any religious materials. I had surrendered these to the authorities long ago.

Finally, at about 2:00 in the morning, they gathered up

our clothing and other belongings to take with them. But before they left, they posted a sign on our door that said the two of us were to do manual cleaning work every morning for the alley. With our health the way it was, we had no idea how we would carry out these orders.

When the principal of Li-Mei's school heard she had to do manual labor, he could not believe it. He immediately wrote a letter to the authorities on her behalf. Not long afterward, the order was rescinded, and all our possessions were returned.

Spared from disability

One afternoon we received a notice saying that everyone in our alley had to assemble at the local Communist party office at 7:00 a.m. the next day.

The next morning we were all there, wondering what was going on. After a while, one of the officers led us to a big theater. Once inside, we knew we had been brought there to be punished. The leading member of the Red Guard of our neighborhood beat us with a bamboo stick, while scolding us, saying, "This is the result of following the subversive policy of Liu Xiao Chi and Deng Xiao Ping."

I did not know what the Liu and Deng policy was, but it did not matter. Not only were we beaten, they even cut our hair. A friend had given me a Swiss watch years ago. When I had first been put into prison several years ago, it had been taken from me. When I left, though, it was returned. As I was being beaten, I was hit on the wrist, but the watch took the blow. It was broken to pieces, but my hand was preserved.

Again, I saw how God had taken care of me, even in the smallest detail. That morning I had debated whether or not I should wear my watch. I have no doubt that if I had not have worn it, my left hand would have been broken. My right hand had been disabled by my earlier paralysis, and I used my left hand for everything.

After my beating, I was dragged on stage in front of everyone and made to kneel down. Finally, they let us leave.

At home I told Li-Mei, "Thank the Lord, I do not feel any pain." That night as I changed to my sleeping clothes, I discovered my body was black and blue all over. Yet, I still did not feel any pain.

The next day the punishment and humiliation continued. We were ordered to attend another public accusation for the sake of our "reeducation." My back was terribly sore by this time, and by the third day the pain was so severe that I could not get up from bed. I stayed in bed for a full month.

But that day I received a promise from the Lord, and I put the words (from Ezekiel 34:26-31) to music.

> I have made a covenant of grace with you/ to rid the land of wild beasts,/ So that you may live in the desert/ and not be devoured by the wild beasts./ I am the Almighty God Jehovah/ who leads you by a pillar of cloud,/ At night I lead you by a pillar of fire/ to protect you as the pupil of my eye./ I will bless you and your surrounding places,/ that life-giving water will always flow./ I will also send showers of blessing,/ and bless you as the dew drops from heaven./ The trees of the field will yield their fruits,/ and the ground will yield its crops./ You will be secure in your land,/ and no longer be plundered by the nations./ I will break the bars of your yoke,/ and rescue you from those who enslave you./ You will no longer be the scorn of the nations,/ nor will you be their victim anymore./ I will provide for you a land renowned for its crops,/ so that you will no longer be victims of famine./ I am the Lord

your God who is with you,/ to protect and watch
over you forever.

14

Living Under
Communist Rule

This on and off questioning and punishment continued. It was, I suppose, intended to accomplish my reeducation. One morning two officers came to inform me that I had to report to the cultural center that afternoon. My heart felt as if it was weighted down with a big stone, and I wondered if I was going to receive another beating.

When I got there, I, along with several others, was made to stand facing a wall. Just then I heard the Heavenly Father's voice: "Do not fear, for I am with you" (Isaiah 41:10). His peace washed over me, and I felt comforted and relaxed.

About half an hour later, I was called in for questioning. They only asked me a few questions and seemed to be satisfied with the answers. They dismissed me, and I walked out to the yard with bowed head.

It was extremely hot that day, and after a bit, the person on my right fainted. Because my head was bowed, I could not see what they were doing to her, but I heard what they said: "You are just putting on an act! Look, this person standing next to you is much older than you, and she can take it. Get up!"

After this, we were allowed to leave. I went home in a

hurry and told Li-Mei what had happened that day—and especially about how God spoke words of comfort to me. To those who fully trust in Him, His promises will be fulfilled. The experience at the cultural center was a testimony from beginning to end that God is faithful and dependable. "I will not violate my covenant/ or alter what my lips have uttered" (Psalm 89:34). "O LORD Almighty,/ blessed is the man who trusts in you" (84:12). Fellow believer, is there anything burdening your heart? Put all your trust in the Lord. Everything that happens has His perfect purpose. When the day He has appointed comes, you will see the workings of His mighty power!

Another public accusation

Five years later, I again was summoned to report to the local Communist committee to be criticized and accused. Relying on God's grace, I went before my accusers. My heart was calm as a baby asleep on his mother's breast. This time I thought the accusations against me would be less severe than before. But I was wrong.

I was led into the meeting hall with a sign attached to my forehead. It proclaimed that I was a counterrevolutionary. At first I was asked several ordinary questions: "What is the source of your living expenses?"

"My friend Li-Mei Tu helps me out," I replied.

"Why would she do that?"

"Because I helped her until she graduated from college."

My studies in America and my trips to Europe and the Holy Land were offered as evidence of my antigovernment activities. And I was put on trial.

As I stood there, one charge was piled on another, and I was branded a criminal guilty of the worst crimes. The crowd—

all Communist sympathizers—demanded that I be sentenced to manual labor. In the past, because my illnesses were known to the authorities, I was not sentenced in such a manner. This time was different.

Hard labor

I was convicted and sentenced to perform manual labor in our alley. I was to start the next day. My responsibilities included cleaning the sewer, scrubbing the bathrooms at the public offices and making sure there was fresh drinking water. Besides these I had to sweep the streets.

I tried to do my best, but my health often prevented me from performing up to the party's "standards." But what was worse was the mean pranks the Red Guards played on me and the foul language they used in speaking to me.

I bowed my head in submission and continued with my work. However, I did find help when things got too bad. Some local Army officers always seemed to take a stand for what was right. For example, one afternoon I cleaned the bathrooms, the Red Guards insisted that it was not clean and wanted me to do the work over. An Army officer spoke up and said, "She has already cleaned it. There is no need for her to do it again."

Another time, when I was sweeping the street, a boy began throwing stones at me. I told him to stop, but he would not. One of the officers happened by and forced him to stop. He even told his parents about the incident, and the next day the boy's mother came to apologize. God was working in small ways to vindicate me.

Other people, though, expressed the exact opposite attitude. In fact, they encouraged their children to humiliate me, saying, "She deserves such treatment because she is a counterrevolutionary."

Some people let their chickens out on the places I had

just cleaned. Others deliberately poured their charcoal ashes down the toilets, which caused the sewer to back up. Still others scattered their garbage along the street on their way to the garbage bin. They thought it was fun to pull tricks on an old woman.

I write this not to recall the wrongs of people, but to let the reader know that the Lord was my strength during these times. He helped me finish my daily tasks and to endure the taunts and pranks. "I can do everything through him who gives me strength" (Philippians 4:13). "We are more than conquerors through him who loved us" (Romans 8:37).

I should also mention that God brought many kind people my way. One day while cleaning the sewer, I had to lift a heavy pail filled with human waste. A woman came by, saw my dilemma and offered to help me lift the bucket. On another occasion I was carrying a bucket of water and tripped. I tried my best to stand back up, but I kept falling down. The same woman came and helped me to my feet, then carried the bucket for me.

Li-Mei helped me the most. She bought all the tools I needed to do my work. And she provided daily encouragement for me.

The Lord works in my behalf

One time, Li-Mei told me, "Your heart is so big. I could never do what you are doing."

"My attitude is not natural," I told her, "it comes from the Heavenly Father. He helps me to manifest the attitude of Christ in all I do."

When I was a child, I could recite from memory a book titled *Progress Reader*. There were many sayings in it that stuck in my mind. One was "Kindness will be repaid by kindness; evil will be repaid by evil." However, the Bible tells us, "Do not repay anyone evil for evil" (Romans 12:17), and "'It is mine to avenge; I will repay,' says the Lord" (verse 19). This was my consolation during these rough days.

There was one person who had contributed to the criminal charges brought against me. As the years went by, the suffering she experienced more than equaled the misfortune she caused me. Her husband became the object of criticism in the factory where he worked, and he lost his job. From there the woman's fortunes in life spiraled downward. Next, her husband was charged with misdeeds and brought to trial. He was branded a public enemy. She became so distraught that she attempted suicide. Were it not for the kindness of her neighbors, she would have died.

When all this happened, my troubles from her suddenly ended. This showed clearly who was behind the charges against me. From that time on, when I was working in the streets, her two sons never bothered me. Surely, God had taken the responsibility to fulfill His promise to avenge wrongdoing against His children.

But there was something I had to do. Verse 20 in Romans 12 says, "'If your enemy is hungry, feed him; / if he is thirsty, give him something to drink.'" So after this woman's failed suicide attempt, I visited her in the hospital. I told her that I did not hate her. Because of God, I could love her, and I wanted her also to know His love.

Almost forced to move

Early one morning I said out loud in a dream, "Hallelujah! Praise the Lord! He let me go over this high mountain. Isn't it amazing?"

Li-Mei awakened me and asked if I was OK. I told her, "In my dream I saw myself standing in front of a very high mountain and thought, *This mountain is too high. I could never climb it.*

But in the twinkling of an eye, I was lifted up and over the mountain, as if I were flying. God seems to be telling me that victory is ahead."

After performing my work for the day, I did not feel well. I checked my temperature and found that I was running a fever of 102 degrees. So I went to bed.

About 10:00 that night, I heard the sound of steps on the stairs. It was the building manager, and he wanted us to move to another apartment. Li-Mei told him we did not want to move, but it did not help. We had three days to be packed and out. (If I had not been ill, we would have had to move immediately.) We had no choice but to obey; after all, I was a counterrevolutionary. Then it dawned on me: this was the mountain in my dream, and somehow, God would help us cross over it.

On the third day, Li-Mei took a letter of petition to the manager. In it she said, "Please do not make us move. We both are weak and often sick, and it would not be fitting for us to move to the bottom part of the building where it is damp."

After he read the letter he told Li-Mei, "I don't care about your condition. You have to move." Li-Mei came back dejected and told me what he had said.

The next day, my fever receded, and I went back to my duties. That afternoon, when I reached the apartment, the Lord said to me, "You do not have to move. He will not come." I did not tell Li-Mei what the Lord had said, but I wrote it on a piece of paper and tucked it away for safe keeping.

The next day was Sunday, and when I went out to do my work, I saw the mother and child of the family that moved out of the apartment we were to move into. They were moving back into their old apartment! Something had caused them to change their minds about moving to our apartment. As a result, our eviction notice was canceled.

At that news, I took out the paper I had put away and read the words to Li-Mei. We gave thanks and praised the Lord for the way He worked.

15

Life Draws to a Close

Early spring in 1970, two snowstorms hit Shanghai one after the other. The government issued a call to the people to help clear the snow. I gladly joined the snow-clearing team, even though I was not able to do much work. I did put out a lot of perspiration, though!

Along with six other people, I still had responsibility for helping to clean and sweep the streets in my alley. When Li-Mei was not sick, she, too, helped out. But one day the work became too much for me, and I fell ill. My fever reached 104 degrees.

At first, I did not want to see a doctor. I hoped that I soon would get better. But when I did not, I had to go to the hospital. The doctor discovered that I had a serious case of pneumonia and gave me medication.

Two weeks later, when I failed to recover, the doctor brought me back in and took some X-rays. They showed that my right lung was decreasing in size, which probably meant that I had cancer. I was referred to the Tumor Medical Center. The doctors there made it clear that because of my age, I would not be able to undergo the necessary treatment. They made it clear that I should go home and let nature take its course. I knew what they meant. If I had been 20 years younger, they would have done their best to heal me. But I was 70 years old.

All I could do now was depend on Jehovah who had delivered me from death numerous times in the past. He is the Father who loves me, the Almighty God! I am His child. Would He not care for me?

I got well slowly. After a year and 10 months, I resumed my work in the streets. Praise His name!

Dead in two minutes

On the morning of January 28, 1975, Li-Mei went to the market to buy food. After bringing her parcel home, she went out again to buy soap at a different store. By the time she returned, she was feeling tired and wanted to rest. The two of us had been taking turns being sick—we two old ladies were a sight!

Li-Mei was in charge of buying food and other household necessities, and I had the responsibility of cooking and cleaning.

She often told me, "If a person dies at age 60, it is not too short a life." Every night before she went to sleep she often prayed, "Dear Lord Jesus, I pray that when my time to die comes, it is quick. Let me quickly depart from this world so that I will not be a bother to Yuen-Lin. She is in poor health and will not be able to take care of me." The Heavenly Father answered her prayer. On that day she returned from shopping, she lay down to rest and was dead in two minutes.

It was a shock, but what could I do? After all, this was her wish and prayer. Many of the local Communist committee members and her former students attended the funeral. The sincerity of the local committee members and the way they handled her left a deep impression on me. No doubt, her Christlike life left an impression on them.

Not long after Li-Mei died, I was faced with moving. Several people wanted my apartment—my home for 22 years—and I was only one old woman.

Naturally, I feared moving to a new place. Friends and neighbors were concerned that I would have no one to care for me. But as always, the Lord was my helper. I knew that He would look after me.

My new place was not bad, and I quickly got to know the neighbors. When they saw me cleaning, they said, "You are old and your health is poor. You should not be doing this work. We will do it for you."

Love for singing

I could not do much for Jesus in my old age, but I could do one thing—praise Him! I often did this by singing hymns, something I have loved to do since I was a child. Besides praising God, it helped me to get rid of boredom.

Not only do I love to sing, the Lord has blessed me with the talent for writing songs. During the five years of my house arrest, I relied on reading the Bible and ancient literature and writing hymns to pass the time. To date, I have written 300 hymns and set them to music. Half are based on the Psalms, and many are from the eight chapters of the Song of Songs, which has supplied me with enough material to write 150 hymns.

A final thank you!

The side effects of my paralysis cause my right hand to shake, making it difficult for me to write. But God has held my shaky hand as I have written down my life story. Indeed, as I look back over my life, one thing stands out more than any other—He has held my hand through all of life. Never did He leave me; never did He forsake me. My innermost being is moved to cry out "Hallelujah!"

And now, to all those who have shown concern for the orphanage, my many friends and doers of good deeds, I want to extend my heartfelt gratitude. You were generous, continuing your financial support from the beginning of the orphanage to the time the government took it over—17 years! May all the glory be to the Father in heaven!

Editor's Note: Yuen-Lin Wu went to be with her Lord in 1982 at the age of 82.